STORY - TELLING LESSONS

By

HENRY EDWARD TRALLE, M. A., Th. D.

———

PHILADELPHIA

THE JUDSON PRESS

BOSTON   CHICAGO   ST. LOUIS   LOS ANGELES
KANSAS CITY   SEATTLE   TORONTO

FOREWORD

THIS volume is one in a series of texts in religious education known as the " Judson Training Manuals for the School of the Church."

These manuals are arranged in three groups, namely, general, departmental, and parent-training. The *general* group includes vital teaching, story-telling, church-school buildings, expression through worship, handwork, community service, educational leadership, appreciation of the Bible, and kindred worth while themes in the field of religious education. The *departmental* group covers courses for every department of the school of the church—Cradle Roll, Beginners', Primary, Junior, etc. The *parent-training* manuals emphasize religion in the home, and the necessity of training for the God-given, heaven-blessed privilege of parenthood.

It is the aim of these manuals to popularize the assured results of the best psychology and pedagogy, and to make them the willing and efficient servants of all workers in the school of the church.

Both the editors and the writers want these books " to live where the people live," and to be of real value to those forward-looking folks destined to be the leaders in religious education.

To this end, each course will be (1) simple in language; (2) accurate in statement; (3) sound in psychology; (4) vital in pedagogy; (5) concrete in treatment; (6) practical in purpose; and (7) spiritual in tone.

This book on "Story-Telling Lessons" will be welcomed by all teachers, preachers, and parents. It is the simplest and sanest presentation of this most valuable form of teaching.

It puts story-telling artistry upon the market in attractive fashion. The book is packed full of teaching values.

Doctor Tralle, the author, is a master in religious education. He has a rare combination of high-grade scholarship and ability to put truth in virile, every-day English.

In Chapter I, he handcuffs the reader's interest and holds it captive to the end.

W. EDWARD RAFFETY.

CONTENTS

Order Number 736-0271780-5312128   Supplied by GB Books

Catalogue Number   Title and Artist   Qty

= 9781419113796 Story Telling Lessons [Paperback] by Tralle, Henry Edward   1

Some items may be shipped separately

Order Processed: 8/29/2008 1:50:00

Payment has been received from: Jon Orchard

Email Address: jonmonkeys@msn.com

RETURNS: Return the item with this despatch note to the following address: Paperbackshop Ltd, Unit
22 Horcott Industrial Estate, Horcott Road, Fairford, GLOS, GL7 4BX, UK . Please tick one reason for
return:

1. [ ] Damaged   2. [ ] Faulty   3. [ ] Wrong Item   4. [ ] Other

CHAPTER I

LEARNING STORY-TELLING

No, story-tellers are not born. They are made. Of course some are more easily made than others, chiefly for the reason that they were more fortunate in their early environment and unconscious training. Fortunate are those individuals who were taught, early in life, to see clearly and to feel deeply, and then to get others to see and feel what they themselves have seen and felt. They become the best story-tellers.

HOW LEARN STORY-TELLING

Anyone of average ability may become an efficient story-teller if he is willing to pay the price in intelligent, persistent effort, under competent direction. Some specific suggestions are here presented.

1. Study Principles of Story-telling

This book is an attempt to present the fundamental, psychological principles of story-telling, with practical suggestions regarding the art of story-telling, and to do this in a fresh, stimulating way. The author is greatly indebted to the story-tellers whom he has heard and whose books he has read, but at the same time he feels that he is not presumptuous in taking issue with some of their statements and in advancing some new view-points, since he has had twelve years' experience in teaching classes in

1

story-telling in college and training-school and in telling stories to a variety of audiences in various sections of our country.

Some of the best books, dealing with the principles and the art of story-telling, are the following: " The Use of the Story in Religious Education," Eggleston; " The Art of the Story-Teller," Shedlock; " Educating by Story-Telling," Cather; " For the Story-Teller," Bailey; " Manual of Stories," Forbush; " Story-Telling in School and Home," Partridge; " Stories and Story-Telling," St. John; " How to Tell Stories to Children," Bryant; " Stories and Story-Telling," Keyes; " Story-Telling," Lyman; " Telling Bible Stories," Houghton; " Some Great Stories and How to Tell Them," Wyche; " Children's Stories and How to Tell Them," Esenwein and Stockard; " Story-Telling for Upper Grade Teachers," Cross and Statler.

Of course no book, or books, ever can take the place of the living teacher, and always it is advisable to study story-telling under a good teacher, if this is possible, in addition to reading the books. At the same time, it is possible to learn story-telling without a teacher, through the reading of the books and by persistent practice.

2. Read Many Good Stories

Unfortunately, there are not many books of stories which conform to the fundamental principles of good story-telling, but at the same time there are a number of books which present fairly good examples. It is advisable to read a great number of these stories, and to read them critically, in connection with a study of the basic principles.

Some of the best examples of story-telling may be here indicated. Some representative books of stories are the following: "For the Children's Hour," Bailey and Lewis; "The Golden Spears," Leamy; "Stories to Tell Children," Bryant; "Golden Windows," Richards; "Old Stories of the East," Baldwin; "Tell Me a True Story," Stewart; "Blue Fairy Book," Lang; "Descriptive Stories for All the Year," Burnham; "Fairy Tales a Child Can Read and Act," Nixon; "Five Minute Stories," Richards; "Story-Tell Lib," Slosson; "Ethics for Children," Cabot; "Worth While Stories for Every Day," Evans. A book that contains a considerable quantity and variety of story materials, though the form in which the stories are presented cannot be regarded as at all ideal, is "World Stories Retold," by Sly.

3. Hear Expert Story-tellers

Valuable suggestions may be had from listening to experienced story-tellers. It is advisable, moreover, to hear as many different story-tellers as possible, since there will be less likelihood of imitation.

As the student listens to story-telling, he should give himself up to its lure, listening attentively and sympathetically. Then he should carefully analyze the story-telling to which he has listened in the light of his study of the fundamental principles of good story-telling.

4. Practice Story-telling Persistently

One of my students, Jane Willis, was asked to tell a story in class for criticism, early in the course, and she reluctantly agreed to do so.

When she came to the telling of the story, she was greatly embarrassed, and gave us about the poorest example of story-telling I had ever heard. I made a few suggestions as to how she might improve her story-telling, and asked her to tell the story again, at the next meeting of the class. I said, " You will do better next time."

The next time she did a little better, but seemed frightened, and was evidently discouraged. I said to her: " Your chief difficulty is lack of self-assurance. Try to forget yourself. See what is going on in your story. Lose yourself in it. Now, try that story again, the next time we meet." She said: " Oh, I cannot do it. I just cannot tell a story." I saw that she was about to cry, and said nothing more to her at the time.

At the close of the class she came to me, saying, " I feel that I am carrying too much work in the school, and I am going to drop story-telling." I said, " You may drop anything else, but you are not going to drop story-telling." She said, " But I can never learn to tell a story." I said, " Yes, you can. Just make up your mind that you will, and stick to it."

I feared that she might not be present at the next meeting of the class, but she was there. Two weeks later she told another story in the class, and did better. From that time on she steadily improved in her story-telling. Toward the end of the course I said, " I have here a clipping from a newspaper which has in it, it seems to me, the making of a good story. I should be glad to have some member of the class take this clipping and work it over, arranging it in good story-telling form, embodying all the principles of a good story, and then tell it in the class."

The first one to volunteer to undertake this difficult task was the young woman who had declared she never could become a good story-teller. She said, " I can try it if you want me to." I said, " You are the very one to do this. I had hoped that you, of all the members in the class, would be the one that would be willing to undertake it."

At a later meeting of the class, when she had finished telling the story that she had prepared, in accordance with my request, she was spontaneously and vigorously applauded, and one of the other members of the class said, " Why, that is the best story we have had in this class."

I said, " You are right; it is, without question, the best example of story-telling we have had in the class."

" Thank you, Miss Willis."

WHY LEARN STORY-TELLING

" Let me tell the stories, and I care not who writes the text-books," says G. Stanley Hall; and, more recently, William Byron Forbush has said: " Of late we have come to take story-telling seriously. It is one of the oldest of arts, and one of the most valuable."

1. Stories Have Great Cultural Value

" Stories are the oldest form of transmitted culture, and the most formative," says Richard G. Moulton. " Is it not delightful to note that learning is bringing the adult back to the story?" So says Angela M. Keyes. And again, Edward Porter St. John: " The loss of a love for stories may be the result of sophistication, but it is not an evidence of wisdom. To feel contempt for their use reveals ignorance of the art of education."

Story-telling is as truly cultural, as really educative, as is Latin, Greek, mathematics, art, music, or any other curriculum subject. There are no choice studies, or subjects, which have an exclusive cultural value, and the number of " cultural subjects " in the curricula of our schools has increased amazingly during the last twenty years.

A prominent educator, in a convention address, said: " I could have remained in the university one year longer, after having received my A. B. degree, and could have taken every subject in the curriculum, which was constructed on the theory that there were a limited number of subjects which possessed a peculiar cultural value. The graduate was supposed to be educated in general, but was not fitted for anything in particular. Now the curriculum has been enlarged to such an extent, through the addition of a great number and variety of subjects, in which are included story-telling and home economics, that the taking of all the subjects in the enlarged curriculum by my daughter, who is just entering this same university, would take two hundred forty years out of her sweet young life."

It is gratifying to note that *story-telling is coming into its own in the schools as a recognized method of making effective important cultural values,* and we are coming to realize that it has been the story-telling outside the formal processes of the schools to which we have been indebted for a very considerable proportion of our real education. The story has been quietly putting control into life.

It is a hopeful indication that we are coming more

and more to realize that it is through story-telling artistry that we may hope most effectively to pass on to future generations the cultural treasures of advancing humanity. The story makes effective the highest ideals of life.

Story-telling appeals strongly to the whole individual in the three phases of consciousness, namely, the intellect, the emotions, and the will. The story makes a particularly strong appeal to the imagination, which is the function of mind through which we are enabled to obtain a sense of reality. Also the story appeals strongly to the feelings, or emotions, developing a sense of spiritual values, or an appreciation of the best things in life. So also, through the story, the will is strengthened most effectively, and right choices are developed.

2. Stories Aid in Understanding History

The history of every people begins with stories, and, in all history, it is the stories that most deeply impress us and influence us, and not names, dates, and mere facts. It is the stories which may be said to contain and to transmit the spiritual values of history, and to make them practically effective in posterity.

It is not their annals that have revealed the peoples of the world to us, but their stories. We best know the Greeks through the Homeric and other stories, the Romans through Plutarch's Lives, and the Hebrews through the stories of the Bible; and these are the three peoples who have given to the world its three best gifts, namely, culture, law, and religion.

We did not get our truest and strongest impressions of the World War from statistical tables and official reports, but from stories. The best transcript of American contemporary life is not to be found in census reports, economic essays, or didactic editorials, but in the stories of the novelist, the short-story writer, the moving-picture producer, and the skilful story-teller. We learn history, and teach it, most effectively when it is done dramatically, and not didactically.

3. Stories Make Education Interesting

Most of us have been guilty of sitting up the greater part of a night in order to finish reading a story, but who ever committed such indiscretion in the reading of essays, editorials, sermons, or commentaries, unless it were a matter of duty or compulsion? And we read stories, instead of listening to them, only because there are more story-books than there are story-tellers. Any story is, of course, far more interesting and effective when it is artfully told than when it is read.

In the story, education assumes the guise of entertainment, and it accomplishes its more serious purpose most effectively because it does entertain incidentally. The story does not argue for a "soft pedagogy," but for a vital pedagogy. The story makes learning a delight, and why should it not be so?

It is a harmful educational superstition to believe that the way to make learning effective is to make it difficult. There will remain enough of the difficult for Soldier Student, in the educational front line, after Red Cross Story has applied all her antiseptics and bandages, and has served all her sandwiches and sweets and hot drinks.

A student said to a certain teacher: "I'd come to your class just for recreation if I didn't learn a thing, but I do learn a great deal. I never had any teacher to make me think for myself as you do, and to so inspire me to better life and service." She was talking to a teacher who had learned how to vitalize the teaching period with a dramatic telling of appropriate stories.

4. Story-telling as a Humanizing Process

It would be difficult to overestimate the value of the story as a humanizing and socializing agency. It is a cure for false dignity and excessive individualism. It gets one out of his own little world into the great, broad world of all humanity. It brings one into contact with every phase of human life and activity. *It leads one to become interested in other people, and to become more generous, more charitable, more cooperative.*

While the story is accomplishing its socializing effects, it is doing the chief thing that we are trying to do in our modern education. Indeed, one of our representative leaders in religious education, Professor T. G. Soares, has defined education as follows: " Education is a scientifically directed process of progressively developing socialized personality."

This socializing of personality is accomplished most effectively through the story for the reason that the listener has presented to him socialization in action. That is, he sees human beings, in the story, behaving toward one another as they ought, and so he himself tends to behave as he ought toward other individuals through the dramatic suggestion of right human relationships in action. In case the individual in a story does not behave as he should toward other individuals, such behavior is made unattractive to the listener.

READING AND DISCUSSION

1. Discuss the story of Jane Willis.

2. Quote five sentences from the following references, and indicate, in a sentence, your reason for the selection made in each case: Keyes, pages 3-12; St. John, Introduction and Chapter I; Partridge, pages 3-28; Sly, Chapter I; Wyche, pages 1-10; Forbush, Chapter I.

3. Give a brief summary of Chapter XIII in Partridge.

4. Give a brief summary of Chapter XIII in Forbush.

5. See discussions of recreational value of story-telling in the following: Wyche, pages 31-39; Bryant, pages 19, 20; Forbush, page 4; Partridge, page 79.

6. Note what Henry Ward Beecher did with a story on one occasion. See Sly, pages 4, 5.

7. In considering the socializing value of the story, read Partridge, page 73, and Forbush, Chapter XIV.

8. Tell a story in the presence of someone in whom you have confidence, courting frank criticism, and then re-tell the story, seeking to profit by the criticisms which have been made. The oftener the same story is told, the more will the story-teller profit in the telling, and the more effective will be the story with others.

9. Professor Hugh Hartshorne has said, in effect, in a public lecture, that the function of the religious educator is (1) to guide the child in purposeful activity, (2) to assist him in social functioning, (3) to control his environment, and (4) to aid him in the experiencing of God. And he adds that this process of education is best facilitated by teaching-stories, which motivate behavior, visualize standards of conduct, and rationalize and modify experience. Discuss.

CHAPTER II

TELLING THE STORY

However good the story may be in itself, and however perfect its form, it must be well told in order to be effective. The main thing in story-telling is the telling.

1. Strive to Appear at Ease

The appearance of ease in the story-teller tends to give the impression of power, of competency, of mastery of the situation, and enables the listener to devote his whole attention to the story itself.

(1) Hands and Feet

The hands should be in repose, at the sides of the body, except when used in gesture, in order that they may not attract attention. To have the hands in the pockets, to hold one with the other, in front or at the back, or to hold on to a book, paper, or table, likely will tend to attract attention to the story-teller rather than to the story. Therefore control the hands.

As to the feet, ordinarily they should be rather close together, with one a little in advance of the other, with an occasional, but not too frequent, shifting of positions. Sometimes, of course, the action of the story will require an altogether different placing of the feet and hands. The aim should be to make both the feet and the hands as inconspicuous as possible, but sometimes this is best accomplished by using them in appropriate gesture.

11

(2) Direction of the Gaze

The story-teller should look at his audience, without appearing to look at any particular individual, and at the same time he should not shift the direction of his gaze too frequently, as this indicates lack of self-control, and will attract attention to the story-teller. In impersonation, the story-teller should direct his gaze as would the character in the story, and, in changing from one character to another, a shifting of the gaze will assist in distinguishing between the characters.

Always, the story-teller should be careful to observe the "angle of vision," being careful not to look too far to the right or to the left, for the reason that a part of the listeners may not be able to see his face or to understand his words. The angle of vision is about a right angle, so the story-teller should not direct his gaze outside the fourth of a circle.

(3) Standing or Sitting

As a rule, the story-teller should stand in telling a story, unless the circumstances make this impracticable, as when the group is very small, for the reason that one has more freedom for expression when standing than when sitting. In telling stories to very small children, it may be advisable to remain seated, if the group is small.

There would seem to be no good reason for assuming, as some do, that the ideal situation for good story-telling is an evening group in front of an open fire, with only the dim light of the fire for illumination, and the story-teller seated with the others. Such a situation was favorable to story-telling in the olden times simply because it was a situation of relaxation from the toils of the day and of freedom from distractions.

The better situation for good story-telling today is a well-lighted, properly ventilated room with the listeners comfortably seated and the story-teller standing.

2. Giving the Impression of Well-being

The story-teller should appear to be happy. He should smile occasionally during the telling of the story, whenever a smile will not contradict the story, and usually just before beginning.

(1) Intentions Are Good

A happy appearance tends to create the impression that the story-teller means well by his audience, indicating good will, friendliness, and evokes an attitude favorable to the story-teller and therefore to the story itself. An appropriate smile is suggestive of good intentions and is indispensable to the best success in story-telling.

(2) Has Something Good

The story-teller who looks happy suggests by his appearance that his story is a good one, that it will be enjoyable, and that it will benefit his listeners. Of course the story-teller should not smile excessively. His smile should not develop into a chronic grin, but at the same time he should realize that it is of the highest importance to smile frequently, whenever at all appropriate, that he may thus convey the impression, however unconscious his listeners may be of it, that he has something good for them in his story. Keep Happy Smile in your heart-family and as a frequent visitor in your face-family.

3. Realize Vividly the Events

The story-teller must first realize the events of the story, must see each part of the action clearly and vividly, if he would get his listeners to see, to feel, and to will. That is, he must appeal strongly to the imagination, compelling his listeners to see clearly, to image accurately, to have a sense of reality.

(1) Use the Imagination

In order to appeal to the imagination of the listeners, the story-teller must make a right use of his own imagination. The characters in the story should be very real to him. He should be able to see them as actually present. He can succeed in doing this by willing to do it, by realizing that it is essential to success, by using pictures, diagrams, and descriptions, by utilizing all the information available. Nothing in story-telling will be real to the listeners until it is first real to the story-teller.

(2) Yield to the Lure

The story-teller must conscientiously and definitely give himself up to the lure of the story if he would succeed in entrancing his listeners. He should get into the world of the story if he would transport his listeners into its world and lead them about at his will. *The story-teller himself must be first entranced if he would entrance, must be lured if he would lure, must be captivated if he would captivate.*

He is not undertaking to recall words, or indeed to bring anything out of the past into the present, but rather he is face to face with actual beings in a new world, and is virtually lost to his actual condition and surroundings. Only thus can a story-teller hope to succeed.

4. Memorize Actions Rather than Words

It is a serious mistake for the story-teller to undertake to memorize, verbally, the words of a story. To do so will bind his imagination, prevent him from seeing the characters in the story, tend to slow up the rate of speaking, to induce hesitation and pauses, and likely will reduce the telling of the story to a more or less mechanical performance.

(1) See Pictures

The story-teller should devote himself to a clear imaging of characters, beings, places, actions, and scenes. In other words, he should memorize pictures rather than words, and should bind all the pictures in all the events of the story into a symmetrical and beautiful whole. Too much emphasis cannot be placed upon this suggestion.

Story-tellers are prone, particularly those whose experience has been limited, to say, "I have to memorize word for word; otherwise I should forget, and could not say anything." This is a mistake.

(2) Trust the Memory

If the suggestion to image clearly and vividly the events of the story is followed, and if the story-teller will read the story over and over again, reading it completely through each time, and then will undertake simply to cause his listeners to see what he sees and to feel what he feels, he will find that he will reproduce, unconsciously and without effort, the very words of the story, and, if he changes the words, these changes will not be material, and in some cases actually will be better than those which he had in the story as he had read it over repeatedly.

Occasionally, of course, it will be necessary to memorize the very words, where there is purposeful repetition or where there is dialect, but, even in these cases, it is likely that a frequent reading will result in exact repetition without definite effort to memorize verbally. The same will hold good in the case of a story in verse, though here more definite effort to memorize verbally may be required.

5. Make Every Word Understood

The story-teller should speak with clear, correct, distinct utterance, so that every word may be understood by every listener, without unnecessary effort.

(1) Speak Distinctly

Anyone who has taught story-telling or public speaking is surprised to find that many individuals cannot articulate correctly and distinctly many of the sounds in the English language, for the reason that they have not been drilled in phonetics at any period of their education.

It is of the highest importance that the story-teller should take training and should develop in himself the ability to utter every element of the language distinctly and to speak all of them in their various possible combinations. If the listener misses a word, because of indistinct utterance, the whole picture of the event may be marred for him, and the story spoiled. Clear, distinct utterance, proper articulation and enunciation, is all too rare. The story-teller's art demands of him the best possible in this respect.

(2) Train the Voice

It is unfortunate when story-telling that is otherwise good is marred by harshness in the voice, nasal tones, undue loudness, incorrect pronunciation, and other defects of utterance, all of which attract attention to the delivery itself and thus make difficult the hearing, understanding, and appreciation of the story itself. Voice culture is a prerequisite for the best story-telling.

Some are far more fortunate than others in this regard. The early training and environment has been favorable to the development of purity of tone, correctness of pronunciation, and accuracy of utterance. Many have unconsciously acquired incorrect habits of breathing and of utterance, and have developed defects in the voice which greatly interfere with the best effectiveness in story-telling.

6. Take Care to Introduce the New

In telling a story, it is highly important to emphasize the new as it appears during the progress of the story in sentence after sentence. Emphasis should be placed upon each idea and word as it occurs for the first time in each particular story, in order that the listener's attention may be attracted particularly to it and that he may be assisted in getting its meaning, and therefore a realization of the action.

This introducing of the new may be done through appropriate gesture, through stronger stress, through facial expression, and through proper modulation of the voice. Take the following extract from the story of "Why the Chimes Rang":

"There lived, in a country far away, a boy named Pedro, and his little brother. They lived in a little town, some miles from a big city.

"The Christmas season was drawing near, and Pedro and his little brother were talking of the beautiful Christmas celebration held every year in the big city, in the big church whose tower could be seen from where they lived on the days when the weather was fine.

"Pedro said, 'Mother saw the beautiful celebration once, and she says that nobody could ever guess all the fine things there are to see and hear. And she says that she has heard that the Christ-Child sometimes comes down to bless the service.'

"Little Brother said, 'I wish we could see this beautiful service this Christmas eve. If we could go, we might see the Christ-Child, too.' And Pedro said, 'Yes, and we could take a gift for the Christ-Child.' Little Brother asked, 'Oh, what could we take?' Pedro answered, 'We could take my little piece of silver that I earned and have been saving.' 'Oh, that would be fine,' said Little Brother."

The following words are "new" and should be emphasized: Lived, far away, boy, Pedro, brother, little town, miles, big city, Christmas, near, talking, celebration, big church, tower, seen, weather, fine, mother, says, guess, fine things, heard, Christ-Child, bless, we, see, gift, what, piece of silver, fine.

7. Be Physically in Earnest

The story-teller will be evidently alive. It is not

enough that the story-teller be morally in earnest; he must be physically in earnest. He must make his earnestness evident. It is not enough that the story-teller be interested, he must manifest his interest. He must make it evident to his listeners, through an animated, enthusiastic telling.

(1) Speak Rapidly

Too many story-tellers speak too slowly. The rate of speech in story-telling should be rapid, on the whole, slowing down occasionally when the action of the story demands it, and even pausing briefly for emphasis occasionally.

It is difficult to speak too rapidly, provided the story-teller speaks distinctly and with proper emphasis and modulation. Of course, in impersonation, the story-teller may occasionally need to speak slowly, if the character impersonated is a slow speaker.

The human mind gets things quickly, and the story-teller needs to move rapidly, from word to word and from sentence to sentence, that he may sketch his mental pictures quickly, else the listeners will get impatient and become inattentive, and thus fail to see clearly, and to feel and act accordingly.

(2) Move Quickly

Quickness of movement indicates life, and life always is attractive. A slow-speaking, slow-moving story-teller cannot be very interesting and effective.

Of course, the story-teller should not appear to be hurried or worried, should not exhibit symptoms of nervousness and lack of self-control, but at the same time he should be mentally alert and physically alive, indicating in every movement that he is interested and that he has something to tell that is of the highest importance.

(3) Emphasize Frequently

This suggestion has to do with force, one element of which is loudness. It is possible, of course, for the story-teller to make too much noise, but the common fault is an excess of quietness. A story-teller cannot speak quietly, mildly, without speaking monotonously and ineffectively. In the introducing of the new, from sentence to sentence, from event to event, there should be frequent expenditure of extra force and an almost continuous variation in the pitch of the tones in meaningful modulation.

(4) Impersonate Correctly

One of the chief explanations of lack of physical earnestness in story-telling is due to the failure of story-tellers to tell the story dramatically, with a large use of direct discourse and with correct impersonations of the various characters in the story. Impersonation will go far toward breaking up monotony in story-telling and toward a physical earnestness that will demand attention, compel interest, aid the imagination, stir the emotions, and storm the will.

(5) Gesture Appropriately

How often have you seen a story-teller stand or sit perfectly still with immobile hands and arms, and with fixed features. There seems to have arisen among voluntary, untrained story-tellers an idea that amounts almost to a superstition, that the story-teller should talk quietly and avoid gesture.

The truth is that the story-teller should make large use of gesture, appropriately reenforcing the words and the modulation. At the same time also the face should be constantly changing in appropriate suggestiveness.

READING AND DISCUSSION

Discuss the following extracts from representative books on story-telling:

1. "Every scene in a story should be visualized until it is as vivid as a painting on a canvas. It must be studied and imagined until it shifts smoothly and rapidly into the succeeding one."—Cather.

2. "When the story has been selected and its message defined, the next step toward preparation for telling it before the class is that of becoming thoroughly familiar with it. This does not imply memorization, for that involves a loss of the spontaneity that is one of the chief charms of story-telling, nor does it involve close attention to details, but rather a thorough grasp of the story as a whole. Having reached a clean-cut definition of the moral of the tale, there must be a clear appreciation of the feelings which are to be stirred, and then a mastery of the general outlines of the events. If the story has strongly impressed one, two or three thoughtful readings will usually secure these results."—St. John.

3. "Such knowledge does not mean memorizing. Memorizing utterly destroys the freedom of reminiscence, takes away the spontaneity, and substitutes a mastery of form for a mastery of essence. It means, rather, a per-

fect grasp of the gist of the story, with sufficient familiarity with its form to determine the manner of its telling. The easiest way to obtain this mastery is, I think, to analyze the story into its simplest elements of plot. Strip it bare of style, description, interpolation, and find out simply *what happened.*"—Bryant.

4. " Instead of memorizing a whole story, word for word, you should come to know it so well that the spirit of it is yours. Become so imbued with the spirit that it comes to be a part of yourself—something that no one can take from you—something that will not evaporate and vanish away with the loss of a mere word. This sort of memorizing is more a familiarizing of one's self with the author's style than actually reducing any of the story elements to memory. By reading the story over and over you unconsciously attract to yourself a diction, a phrasing that belongs to the author and the piece, that just naturally fits into the situations contained in the story."—Cross and Statler.

5. " Before a story can be told, it must be put definitely into form for telling. It must be studied. Often it will be necessary to know more about the situation than the story itself tells. If it is a part of a larger story, the whole should be read. The told story must be strong in color. The teller's mind must hold it, therefore, in a rich content of imagery and feeling so that it may have body, and there may be plenty of the raw material out of which gesture, attitude, quality of tone, and many other more or less unconscious ways of communicating with the hearer, of suggesting scene and mood, are formed."— Partridge.

CHAPTER III

IMPERSONATION IN STORY-TELLING

The dramatic quality should dominate in the story, both in its form and in its actual telling. In helping the listener to see vividly the action of the story, and to feel its power, the good story-teller will make skilful use of voice, face, the whole body.

REPRESENTING THE CHARACTERS

The story-teller must be, in turn, all the characters in the story, in order that he may make them real to his audience.

1. Action More Effective than Words

Frequently an emphasis on a syllable in a word or an inflection in the voice may be far more effective than the word itself, and indeed may even contradict the word. The words of the story alone constitute a mere skeleton.

This skeleton becomes a living, alluring reality when touched by the magic of modulation, and illumined by the light of facial expression, and propelled by the force of appropriate gesture.

In impersonating the characters of the story, it is not meant, of course, that the story-teller will actually appear as his characters appear or that he will imitate them in every movement and sound, but only that he will *imitate certain characteristic movements and sounds,* by way of suggestion. The imagination of the listener will do the rest.

2. Imitation as an Aid to Imagination

In telling the story of " The Boys and The Frogs," the story-teller should imitate the croaking of the big frog. When the listener hears this characteristic sound, he sees the frog. He does not see the story-teller at all. The story-teller has suddenly become transformed for him into a frog, and at the same time he is not conscious of the transformation—he only sees the frog.

It is a mistake, therefore, to contend, as some do, that impersonation attracts attention to the story-teller, for, as a matter of fact, the result is exactly the opposite. *The story-teller who would make himself as inconspicuous as possible must hide behind the characters of the story*, through a dramatic telling. He must not merely *tell*, but *act*. The more action in the telling, provided it be appropriate action, the more will the attention of the listener be attracted from the story-teller to the story.

In almost every story, there is at least *one place where the story-teller may appeal strongly to the imagination*, through the imitation of some characteristic sound or action, and thus assist the listeners to image clearly and vividly the events.

In the telling of " The Ugly Duckling," for example, the story-teller will imitate the quacking of the mother duck and of the little ducklings, the mewing of the cat, the clucking of the hen, the barking of the dog, etc., and will thus bring the ducks and the cat and the hen and the dog into the very presence of the child, so that he is in the story-world for the time being.

The *success of the story* is dependent on the ability of the story-teller to develop in the listeners this sense of reality, and this is practically impossible without impersonation. The beginner in story-telling may say, " I agree that impersonation is desirable, but I do not know how, and I think it is better not to try at all than to fail at it." No, better fail at it than not to try at all.

Even poor impersonation is better than none. Furthermore, any story-teller can learn to impersonate successfully if he will determine to do it, and then practice, practice, practice. Let him learn from those who do it well, and, occasionally, he can take lessons first-hand. For instance, he may learn to imitate the croaking of a frog by listening to the frog itself, the quacking of a duck by listening to a duck, and the dialect of a human character by listening to the original.

3. Relation of Story-telling to Acting

Some of the writers on story-telling make a superficial distinction between story-telling and acting. Good story-telling is not essentially different from good acting.

It is the fundamental aim of both the story-teller and the actor to lend reality to the scenes presented, to *create the illusion of actuality.* Each goes about his task in a different way, but both aim at essentially the same thing.

The story-teller works alone, whereas the actor has the assistance of other actors and of stage-settings, scenery, etc. *The story-teller must play all the parts alone,* without any make-up or other accessories. He is his own stage-manager, and must compel his audience to create all the scenery as he proceeds.

The story-teller impersonates only partially and imitates only certain characteristic actions, leaving the actual creation of the various scenes to the audience, whereas the actor leaves little to the creative imagination of the audience. In a death scene, for instance, the actor will actually fall to the floor, whereas the story-teller will only indicate or suggest the falling.

The story-teller himself does more than the actor, and he compels his audience to do more than does the actor. His aim is the same as that of the actor, as has been said, but his method is the same only up to a certain point.

In " Worth While Stories for Every Day," by Lawton B. Evans, is the following: " Do not be afraid of the dramatic side of narration. Imitate all the sounds that belong to the story, such as the winds blowing, the thunder rolling, a bear growling, a dog barking, etc. Change your voice to meet the requirements of youth and age. Throw yourself heart and soul into the spirit of the narrative, and do not be afraid to take all the parts and to act each one in turn."

4. Story-telling and Reading

I cannot agree with those writers on story-telling who warn the story-teller to beware of the method of the dramatic " reader." The art of the story-teller is even more closely allied to that of the reader than to that of the actor.

Both the reader and the story-teller must play all the parts, must appeal strongly to the imagination, must create the illusion of present reality, must evoke suitable emotions, and must appeal to the will.

The differences between story-telling and reading are differences in aim rather than in method. The purpose of the story-teller is more serious than that of the reader, the aim of the latter being chiefly entertainment, while that of the former is chiefly instruction. The story-teller does entertain incidentally, but he aims primarily to teach, to bring about a change for the better in the life of the listener.

Good story-telling and good reading are essentially one in method. Both are dramatic in form, abounding in direct discourse, and both make large use of impersonation, imitation, gesture. Both are characterized by action, action, action. Neither the story-teller nor the reader will tie himself to a memoriter method, but will seek to see clearly and vividly and to feel strongly, and will trust to the moment for the exact phraseology, except in the case of verse and occasional phrases and sentences.

5. The Expression of Emotions

The successful story-teller must, in impersonation, properly express the various emotions natural to his characters, in order to evoke similar emotions in his listeners. The expression of some of the most common emotions may be indicated as follows: (1) *Fear,* contraction of muscles, shrinking away from, and sometimes a pushing away with the hands; (2) *Anger,* frowning and a narrowing of the eyes, with redness or whiteness in face sometimes; (3) *Pain,* contraction about the eyes, with partial closing; (4) *Disgust,* drawing down of the corners of the mouth, with a turning away sometimes; (5) *Weariness,* relaxation of the whole body; (6) *Remorse,* approximately a combination of weariness and pain; (7) *Delight,* lighting up of the face, clapping of

hands together, jumping up and down; (8) *Pleasure,*
less strong than delight; (9) *Wonder,* gradual opening
of the eyes and mouth; (10) *Surprise,* sudden opening of
mouth and intaking of breath, with throwing up of hands
sometimes; (11) *Indifference,* a raising of the eyebrows
and a tossing of the head; (12) *Haughtiness,* a drawing
up of the body and a looking down upon; (13) *Pride,* a
throwing back of the head and a slight contraction about
the lips; (14) *Impatience,* a quick frowning and a stamping of the foot; (15) *Loneliness,* a relaxation of the
features, with a far-away look in the eyes.

6. Dramatization of the Story

The dramatizing of the story by the listeners has very
great educational value in deepening the impression, in
aiding the memory, and in developing the personality.

In dramatization, there is a larger measure of impersonation, and thus a nearer approach to the method of
the actor, but essentially it is not different from story-
telling, except that a number of individuals share in the
telling.

THE USE OF GESTURE

" Gesture embraces the various postures and motions
of the body; as the head, shoulders, and trunk; the arms,
hands, and fingers; the lower limbs and feet. It is the
language of nature; and hence, like the expression of
the countenance, is a universal language."

1. Gestures Must be Free

The arm and hand must move through ample space,
and the whole body must yield itself in harmony. The

story-teller should seek to avoid " short and strained gestures, with stiffness of the body, and doubtful or timid movements." Back of the gesture there must be confidence, boldness, a letting go of one's self.

Confidence and success in gesture can come only through a cultivation of a willingness to make mistakes, to appear ridiculous if need be, and through constant practice in connection with a study of the fundamental principles involved.

2. Gestures Must be Timely

The action in preparation must be so timed that the " stroke is made with that degree of force which suits the character of the sentiment and speaker, and occurs on the precise syllable to be enforced."

Timeliness is good articulation in gesture. In uttering the sentence, " There he goes," the pointing finger should be at the greatest distance from the body at precisely the same time the word " there " is heard.

If the pointing comes just before or just after the utterance of the word, attention is attracted to the story-teller and his awkwardness. And the result is the same if the gestures are " vague and sawing."

3. Gestures Must be Appropriate

The action of the story-teller must be suited to the action of the story. Gesture must be adapted to the situation and the sentiment in the events of the story, and must seem to be natural, that it may not attract attention to itself, but, at the same time, may strengthen the impression.

Far from appropriate was the gesticulation of the

minister who was accustomed to use only two gestures, and who said, " When the roll is called up yonder, I'll be there," pointing upward on the first syllable of " yonder," and downward on " there."

Gestures may be classified as follows:

(1) *Designative gestures,* which are " used for indicating or pointing out, and for discriminating between different objects." For example, in saying, " Thou art the man," point with the index finger on " Thou." In saying, " I refer the matter to these friends at my right," gesture on " friends " with the right hand supine, palm up.

(2) *Descriptive gestures,* which serve to describe objects and to represent numbers and space. For example, in saying, " The snow covered all the ground," gesture on " ground " with the outward sweep of the prone hand, palm down.

(3) *Assertive gestures,* which help to strengthen assertions. For example, in saying, " God must be obeyed," emphasize " must " by the stretching downward of the supine hand.

(4) *Indicative gestures,* which help to see clearly and to feel appropriately, as placing the hand upon the head in distress, putting the finger upon the lips to enjoin silence, reaching the hands forward in supplication, dropping the head in shame, nodding the head in assent or salutation, bending the body forward in reverence, starting in terror, stamping in authority, clenching the hand in strong determination, the clenching of both hands in vehement declaration, the palms of the hands pressed together in adoration, the clasped hands in earnest entreaty, the folding of the hands in self-abasement, etc.

4. Gestures Must be Graceful

If gestures are free, timely, and appropriate, they will be graceful, being characterized by facility, freedom, variety, and simplicity.

The little child is graceful in his gestures, and expresses himself naturally and appropriately, but, as he grows older, he is likely to become self-conscious and awkward, by reason of a wrong environment and a formal education, and then he must *learn* to speak properly, and to express effectively ideas and emotions with face and gestures.

It is not natural to the average story-teller to be graceful and effective in gesture, and he will need to make it natural for himself by acquiring the fundamental principles and undergoing the necessary practice. This requires courage, determination, and persistence. It is well to practice in front of a mirror.

READING AND DISCUSSION

Impersonate, with appropriate gesture, facial expression, and modulation of voice, the characters in the following extracts from stories:

1. "One day a selfish boy saw a jar of nuts. He put his hand into the jar and grasped as many as his hand could hold. As the mouth of the jar was small he could not pull his hand out, so he became frightened and began to cry, 'I can't get my hand out!' A boy standing near said, 'Take only half as many, and you can easily get your hand out.'"

2. "Once a hungry cow came to a manger full of hay.

But a dog was lying there, snarling and barking, and would not let the cow come near the hay. The cow mooed, 'Mr. Dog, you're selfish; you cannot eat the hay yourself, and you will let no one else have any of it.' "

3. "One day some boys at play were throwing stones into a pond at some frogs. At last one old frog peeped up out of the water and said, 'Boys, why are you so cruel?' The boys said, 'We are only having fun!' The old frog croaked back, 'It may be fun for you, but it is hard on us.' "

4. "One morning, the Wind said to the Sun, 'I am stronger than you are.' The Sun said, 'I know I am stronger than you are.' As they were quarreling over the question, a traveler came in sight. So they agreed to decide the matter by seeing which could first make him take off his coat. Then the Wind began blowing, blowing as fiercely as he could. He nearly tore off the traveler's coat, but the man buttoned his coat up more closely about him and the Wind had to give up beaten. Then the Sun, clearing away the clouds, shot his hottest beams down upon the traveler's back, and he soon threw off his coat. Then the Sun said, 'Wind, you make more noise, but, you see, I am stronger.' "

CHAPTER IV

FORM OF THE STORY

Careful attention needs to be given to the form in which the story is presented, as well as to the manner and method of its telling.

ACTION AND RAPID MOVEMENT NECESSARY

Always, in the story, through every event, there must be "something doing." There is, in the story, little or no place for description. "Description is the portrayal of concrete objects, material or spiritual, by means of language."

Description is concerned chiefly with *things*, whereas the story is concerned with *events;* description deals with *states*, whereas the story represents *actions;* description treats *details*, whereas the story seeks to make a single *impression;* description puts the emphasis upon *seeing*, whereas the story would have us also to *do*.

1. Picture Vividly the Action

Story-telling really is *story-showing*, and not mere telling. Each event in the story must be so presented as to form a word picture, with a strong appeal to the imagination, in order that the listener may form a clear image.

The action in the story, therefore, must be fully pictured, and not briefly indicated, as in allusions, analogies,

33

and most other so-called "illustrations." One story-teller, in "The Runaway Pancake," says: "It was a funny sight to see a man, and a hen, and a rooster, and a duck, and a goose, and a gander, all joining in the chase."

This is an example of bad story-telling. It would be far better to take time to picture each of those named as joining in the chase and crying, "Stop! Stop! Pancake!" so that the listener may see and hear that string of chasers, and then it will not be necessary, of course, to tell him that it is a funny sight. It will be funny to him, without anybody telling him anything, because he sees what is going on, and knows for himself that it is funny.

2. Employ Chiefly Familiar Terms

One story-teller, in telling the story of the visit of the Wise-men to the baby Jesus, said, to five-year-old children, "And the hot sands of the desert crackled under the feet of the camels as they journeyed." The average child would be puzzled by "desert," "crackled," "journeyed," and likely would not be able to form any mental image at all. Another story-teller used the word "regent" in a story for children of about the same age.

"But," they sometimes object, "is not the use of unfamiliar terms in a story a good method of teaching the child English?" "Yes, possibly," I should say, "provided you do not make the dose too big and strong and bitter." The explanation of the detestation of English on the part of some children may be explained on the assumption that it was given to them in old-fashioned "blue mass" doses.

In telling folk-tales, it is necessary usually to modernize them. In "The Runaway Pancake," for instance, it will be advisable likely to convert "fireside" into kitchen, and to reduce the "seven" hungry children to three. So, frequently, in the King James' Version of the Bible, modern terms should be substituted for the less familiar ones of more than three hundred years ago.

3. Omit Unnecessary Words and Phrases

All words and phrases designed to lead the listener to see and feel as the story-teller thinks he ought to see and feel are to be considered as just so much literary clutter. If the events are properly pictured, the listener can be trusted to see and feel as he ought, without any outside help from the story-teller.

It is bad story-telling, as a rule, for the story-teller to say plainly of anything in the story that it was bad or good, funny or sad. Also it is better to omit altogether from the story all the "Well's" and "So's" and "Oh's" and "Children" and "My dear children."

It is quite safe to assume that the listeners have brains, and it is well to understand that they resent the patronizing cant so common in story-telling.

4. Use Simple Language Constructions

No English can be too correct or too beautiful in the story, provided it be simple. Any attempt, however, at "fine writing" will attract attention to the form instead of to the truth itself. The sentences in the story usually should be short, and always they should yield their meaning readily.

One story-teller goes so far astray, in his departure

from directness and simplicity, as to speak of a railroad engine as an "iron horse" and a "conscienceless monster," and of a boy as "some mother's darling little boy."

In one version of "The Bamboo Tree," the first paragraph should be omitted altogether. This paragraph is as follows: "Beneath the gleaming snows of Fuji lay a great forest. There many giant trees grew, the fir, the pine, the graceful bamboo, and the camellia trees. The balmy azaleas and the crinkled iris bloomed in the shade. The blue heavens were fleecy with snowy clouds, and gentle zephyrs caressed the blossoms and made them bow like worshipers before a shrine."

5. Use Purposeful Repetition Occasionally

Purposeful repetition aids the memory, assists in the forming of clear mental images, facilitates the grasping of the significance of the action of the story, and evokes suitable emotions. Rhythmical repetition is particularly effective with the younger listener, and frequently also with adults.

The prophet Amos, in one of his dramatic lessons, in his teaching campaign in Israel, in order to evoke in his listeners a sense of impending doom, repeats eight times, at the beginning of each of the events of his story, only changing the name of the country, the following refrain: "Thus saith Jehovah, 'For three transgressions of Damascus, and for four, I will not turn away the punishment thereof, because,' etc."

6. Choose the Definite in Preference to the Indefinite

In good story-telling, there can be no hesitation, no alternatives, no probabilities. The story must present, in each event, one clear, positive, definite picture. There must be no wavering, no wabbling, no deliberation.

The story, therefore, must avoid such expressions as "probably," "perhaps," "it may be so," "as it were," "either—or," and "possibly." The story-teller may, in the making of the story, hesitate, deliberate, consider, weigh, and question, but, when the story is finished, he must see certain very definite actions, and must cause the listeners to see them as definite and complete, if his story-telling is to carry with it the sense of reality and a result of effectiveness.

DIRECT RATHER THAN INDIRECT DISCOURSE ESSENTIAL

In its written form, the good story is characterized by many quotation marks, for it abounds in direct discourse, the characters doing their own talking, there being a minimum of indirect discourse, wherein the story-teller presents in his own words the substance of what is said by the characters.

1. Makes Strong Appeal to the Imagination

The chief reason for making large use of direct discourse in the story is that it appeals far more strongly to the imagination than does indirect discourse. The fundamental reason why this is true is that an individual seems more real when you look at him than he does when you simply hear somebody tell about him.

In indirect discourse, the story-teller is simply talking about the characters in the story; but in direct discourse, the story-teller is more than a talker—he is a stage-manager, introducting his characters to the audience and allowing them to do their own talking.

2. Presents Teaching as Indirect Suggestion

Usually, in teaching, indirect suggestion is more effective than direct suggestion, for the reason that the resultant change in the pupil's behavior, or activity, is more hidden in the depths of the subconscious, and the individual has a sense of greater freedom, frequently thinking that he is acting wholly on his own initiative.

So the artful story-teller does not make suggestions directly, but rather indirectly through the characters in the story, knowing that his listeners might resent suggestions presented by himself, whereas they are likely to receive them when presented by his characters.

The sayings of Bacon are less familiar to us than those of Shakespeare because he talked too much. Shakespeare did not say anything. He let his characters do the talking, and we are still listening to them. Herein lies the key to the understanding of the artistry of the dramatist, and it is this ability to allow the characters of the story to do the talking that constitutes chiefly the artistry of the real story-teller. The trained story-teller knows that his listeners will listen far more readily to what his characters say than to anything he may say himself, and that they will accept suggestions from his characters when they would not accept them from him.

3. Relieves the Story-teller of Responsibility

The value of the indirect suggestion of direct discourse, as contrasted with the direct suggestion of indirect discourse, is emphasized when the teaching of the story is particularly new or unpalatable and must contend with considerable prejudice in the listeners. Such teaching is more likely to get a hearing when it comes from one of the characters in the story than if it came directly from the teacher, or story-teller.

When the unacceptable teaching is thus presented indirectly, the story-teller assumes the rôle of a reporter rather than exhorter. He is a fellow traveler and spectator, and not one of the "sights." If the listener does not like what he sees in the story-land, he does not hold the story-teller responsible, and thus his vision is not dimmed by beclouding emotions, and he is more likely to see things as they really are, and not as he thought they would be, with the result that the suggestion has a better chance to become effective.

ALL QUESTIONS IN THE STORY ARE DEFECTS

The common practice of injecting questions into the story by the story-teller is to be deplored. The time for questions is after the story has been told; and, even then, they need to be very carefully managed, and sometimes altogether omitted, lest they interfere with the impression of the story.

1. Questions Halt the Action

The action of the story should move forward swiftly and continuously, without interruptions of any kind. Questions are in the nature of interruptions, and they halt the action of the story, when asked by the story-teller. Occasional questions asked by characters in the story are permissible of course, for they are a part of the action of the story itself.

One story-teller stops her story to ask this superfluous question: "Do you think that this was the first time Rebekah had ever been kind in this way?" That which this question is designed to accomplish could be better attained through the action of the story itself. If the aim of the question is to bring out the fact that kindness to her elders must have been developed slowly as a habit, then it would be better art to have some one of the family say, "Rebekah is always doing something nice for older people."

2. Questions Break the Spell

The story may be said to weave a spell about the listener, and this is necessary to its success. Any interjecting question breaks this spell, and the story must begin over again, for the reason that the question causes the listener to become conscious of self and of the story-teller, whereas the whole attention should be centered upon the action of the story itself, if it is to become real and interesting and effective.

In the story of David and Goliath, one story-teller asks, "What could a boy do against a lion?" Let the story itself answer that question, without its being formally asked. Let the story move right along, showing what this boy did against a lion.

So, again, in the same story, appears the following: "Could not God save this boy from the strong man as he did save him from the strong beast?" It is safe to assume that the listener has already raised this question with himself, and that he is willing to let the action of the story answer it, if only it will move along, without these aggravating interruptions.

3. Questions Bind the Imagination

The story lifts the listener up out of his present actual world into a new and wonderful story-world, and, just as he is beginning really to enjoy himself, the bungling story-teller jerks him suddenly back to earth with his interjected question.

A boy would act no more foolishly if he were to jerk his kite back to the ground every five minutes, in order to make sure that it will fly. The informed story-teller can trust the listener to fly, once he is properly started on the wings of a controlled imagination.

4. Questions Distract From the Teaching

Instead of the question helping the listener to get the teaching of the story, as the untrained story-teller mistakenly thinks, it has exactly the opposite effect. Questions almost certainly will turn the attention away from the story, directing the stream of consciousness upon that which is altogether foreign to the purpose of the story.

If the story-teller's question is rhetorical, it may elicit an unexpected answer, and, if he expects an answer, the result likely will be a guessing contest, with wrong answers, while even a correct answer would be in the nature of a distraction. Therefore, beware of question-distractions.

In a New York paper, there was an account of a Long Island school-teacher, who, in telling the story of Little Red Ridinghood, said, " Suddenly she heard a great noise, and what do you suppose she saw standing there gazing

at her and showing all its sharp, white teeth?" One of
the boys answered, "Teddy Roosevelt!"

5. Questions Violate the Listener's Personality

It should be recognized that it is a gross violation of a
fundamental principle of a vital pedagogy to undertake,
by questions, to interfere with the listener's mental processes as he hears the story. Let us trust him, and let
him alone, allowing him to get his own impressions from
the story—to see and feel and do as he pleases.

If the story contains a good teaching, if the events are
arranged in logical order, with suitable beginning and
ending, if it abounds in rapid action, and is skilfully told,
it will hold the attention and will make its own impression, and any questioning of the listener must be regarded as a species of impertinent interference.

READING AND DISCUSSION

1. Re-write the following, taken from a primary quar-
terly: "Our heavenly Father showed his great love for
us by giving us Jesus as his present to the world, and
because he was such a beautiful gift and the people were
so happy about it, they gave presents to each other. Did
you find pictures of any people who praised God for
him in their churches? Have any of you a new little
baby brother or sister in your home? Did anyone send
or bring a present to the baby? The men about whom
I want to tell you brought presents to the little baby
Jesus. They came a long, long journey to give their
presents to him. These men were not related to the
baby, nor did they know Mary and Joseph. How do you

suppose they found out that the wonderful Christ-Child had come? They lived very far away from the town of Bethlehem, where he was born, and there was no way to send telegrams in those days, nor did anyone write them a letter announcing his birth."

2. Criticize, in the light of the principles set forth in this chapter, at least five sentences from five stories.

3. Re-write the following extract from a book of stories: "Children, do you suppose these two had any work to do? Would you be happy if you played all day long? I think not, for 'tis better to feel that there is something for each to do. God gave this first man and woman some work, and what do you think it was? Why, he told them he wished them to take care of the garden, and they must have enjoyed doing this. Perhaps they brought water to give the thirsty plants a drink, picked off the withered petals from the flowers, and trained the vines to run over the trees. Then when they wanted to eat, they had only to gather the fruits and they had a very nice breakfast or dinner without any trouble of cooking. And at night, where do you think they slept? They had no house, you know, and no bed, but perhaps they piled up some leaves beneath a large tree and there they rested as well as if it had been the softest kind of bed."

CHAPTER V
PARTS OF THE STORY

Every story is made up of a beginning, a series of events, and an ending.

EVENTS

The bulk of the story, all except a brief beginning and a briefer ending, is composed of an orderly succession of events, in the last of which is the climax.

1. The Events Are the Parts of the Action

An event is a part of the action of the story, that is, one of the *significant* things which occurred. It is something that took place, that is, a scene which helps to make the impression when the climax is reached. The skilful story-teller will learn to break up a story into its parts, or events, and to name them, much as he would name the " heads " of a speech. Indeed, the story, in itself, is a speech.

Take the familiar " The Ugly Duckling " as an example. This story, as usually told, may be divided into nine events, namely, (1) The hatching of the egg, (2) The mother's emotion, (3) Attitude of brothers and sisters, (4) Flight from home, (5) Disdain of the dog, (6) Ridicule of cat and hen, (7) Lonely and sad during the winter, (8) Experiences appreciation for the first time, (9) Learns that he is a swan, and is happy.

44

2. Orderly Succession of Events is Essential

Much depends on the order in which the events are arranged if the story is to be effective. In " The Ugly Duckling," for instance, the events are so arranged as to make a single definite impression and to teach a lesson in self-respect—patient waiting for recognition.

Let events one and eight exchange places, and the story is spoiled, for, in that case, we should see the ugly duckling appreciated before he is hatched, whereas we must see the hatching of the egg first, and must realize that this duckling is different from the others. Then we must view him in his vicissitudes and must realize that he is unappreciated and mistreated, and, later, we must rejoice with him when he is understood and appreciated, if the story is to be effective.

If, however, events five and six were to be exchanged, there would be no serious injury to the story, for both are designed to assist us in realizing the sad plight of the unappreciated duckling, and to prepare us for the appreciation which comes later in the story.

3. The Last Event is Most Important

It is the last event in any story that is the most important, because it is the last of the events that justifies all that has gone before, and that brings out the significance of all the preceding events.

It is *a mistake to think of the climax as one of the parts of the story*. It is rather that place in the story, in the latter part of the last event, where the point is made, and the truth, or lesson, is taught. Usually, the climax of the story is more effective when it brings out something that has been held back, and evokes the emotion of surprise or wonder.

4. Number of Events is Not Fixed

There is not a fixed number of events that every story must possess. There may be only three events, or there may be thirty-three. The number of events will depend on the materials of the story, the literary type, and the nature of the teaching. Indeed, in some cases, the same story may be quite as effective with one or two events more or less, as in " The Ugly Duckling."

In this story, events one to seven inclusive picture the unfortunate condition of the hero, and enable the child to sympathize with him in his sufferings, and the last two events picture the contrasting appreciation and happiness, and enable the child to rejoice in the happy outcome, and, at the same time, unconsciously to get the teaching.

It is manifest that the first seven events might be reduced to six, or even five, or that the number might be increased to eight, by the introduction of another event showing the ridicule of a cow, for instance, without materially affecting the story's value.

5. Each Event Suggests a Mind Picture

No story can succeed unless it makes a strong appeal to the imagination of the listener. It must lead the listener to image one occurrence after another, and then, when the climax is reached, to see the blending of all these pictures in one mental image. The vividness of this picture will be the measure of the success of the story.

6. The Method of Arranging the Events is Called the Plot

It has been suggested that there are three principal types of plot, or plan of construction, in the making of a story, namely, the one-hero plot, the two-hero plot, and the three-hero plot.

(1) One-hero Plot

In a story with this plan of construction, there is a " single line of sequence," all the action centering in the one individual, as in " The Ugly Duckling." A variation of this type is the " cumulative plan," where there are " repetitions and added incidents," as in " The Runaway Pancake."

(2) Two-hero Plot

In a story with this plan of construction, there are " two contrasting courses of action placed side by side," as in " Diamonds and Toads," and the impression comes from the contrast between the actions of the two individuals, rather than from the contrast between different actions, or experiences, of the same individual, as in the case of the story with the one-hero plot.

(3) Three-hero Plot

In the story with the three-hero plot, there is a " three-parallel line " of action, where there are three contrasting courses of action as in " Boots and His Brothers." The point of the story is made through the contrasting actions of the different individuals. This plan of construction is effective with younger students.

BEGINNING

Every story needs a beginning, or introduction, preceding the first event. The nature of this beginning, and its handling by the story-teller, will very materially determine the success or failure of the story.

1. Its Purpose

The purpose of the beginning of the story may be said to be threefold.

(1) To Get Attention

It is important, at the start, to get attention, to focus the consciousness of the listener upon the story. This is done through a proper beginning form, and also through the method of its delivery by the story-teller—that is, through the proper use of the voice and of gesture.

(2) To Arouse Interest

It is the province of the beginning also to arouse interest in the story itself, through a point of contact with the life of the listener, and the awakening of a curiosity and an expectation of something desirable to come.

(3) To Create an Atmosphere

A good beginning also will create a suitable atmosphere for the story, will induce a mood favorable to the impression of the story, will awaken an expectation in harmony with the story.

In some cases, the beginning may even give a hint as to the nature of the action of the story. However, it is important that the beginning shall not contain any of the action of the story, and that it shall not reveal in advance the point of the story, but that it shall leave it to the listener to discover for himself the meanings as they are shown in the events in the development of the story. The experience of discovery is a delightful one.

2. Its Length

The beginning should be very short. Usually a sentence is sufficient. Some things frequently found in beginnings should be left out.

(1) Descriptions

There should be very little description in the story, and that which is necessary should appear in the events, and not in the beginning. Many stories as they are found in the books and periodicals are sadly marred by long descriptions at the beginning, before interest is aroused in the action of the story itself.

(2) Adjectives

There is scarcely any place at all for adjectives in the story, and certainly not in the beginning. The listener should have the pleasure of finding out for himself whether the hero is good or bad, happy or unhappy, etc. Let the story itself unfold to the listener the action, and let him form his own judgments and experience his own emotions.

(3) Questions

The too common practice of introducing into the beginning questions directed at the listener, with the purpose of connecting the present story with an earlier story or with some other experience in his life, is bad story-telling. Let the story itself do this.

Questions asked for the purpose of getting attention also are bad, for the reason that they actually serve rather as distractions. It is better to get right into the story itself as soon as possible, and to let the story do its own explaining and make its own impression. The story can be trusted to do this.

3. Its Contents

There is no absolute requirement as to what the beginning shall contain, but usually there are found here three things.

(1) Individuals

The individuals with whom the action of the story begins are here introduced. The "individual" may be a human being, a lower animal, or an inanimate object. This individual may be the hero or heroine of the story, and sometimes other individuals are introduced later, in the story itself. The essential is that the beginning shall introduce someone with whom the story itself may start, someone around whom the action will center.

(2) Place

It is essential also, in the beginning, that the place from which the action of the story starts shall be introduced. In " The Ugly Duckling," for instance, it is " nest under a mother duck "; in " The Runaway Pancake," it is " pan " and " fireside," or kitchen; and, in " The Little Red Hen," it is " house in the wood " and " den in the rocks."

(3) Time

The time of the commencement of the story is introduced, in the beginning. Sometimes the exact date is given or the story is specifically connected with some known event—"In the year that King Uzziah died," in the story of Isaiah's vision; "In the winter of 1776," in the story of Washington crossing the Delaware.

Frequently an indefinite time is indicated, as "Once," "One time," "Once upon a time," "There was a time," "One day," "One night," "In the long ago," "Once, nobody knows just when."

Occasionally, an indefinite time is assumed, implied, taken for granted, as "There was," "Three bears lived," "A pancake was frying for supper," "Some eggs were in a nice, warm nest under a mother duck."

4. Its Form

In form, the beginning of the story should be simple, easy, natural. There is no place here for "fine writing," which will attract attention to itself. The language, of course, should be correct, except sometimes in quotations, and it may be beautiful, but it should not be ornate or stilted. This would be true of the story that is to be read, and it is particularly true of the story that is to be told.

The beginning also should be fresh, sincere, out of the ordinary. For example, the stereotyped "Once upon a time" usually should be avoided. Occasionally, the beginning will consist of direct discourse, the words of one of the individuals of the story. This informal method of introduction sometimes is very effective.

ENDING

As soon as the story reaches the climax, at the end of the last event, it must be brought quickly to a conclusion with a suitable ending.

1. Ending Must be Short

The shorter the ending, the better. Usually a single sentence is sufficient. Interest is at its height when the story reaches the climax, and the close must come very quickly, else there will be interference with the impression.

The purpose of an ending is to slow down the stream of consciousness, that attention may be turned back upon the story itself, which is then viewed as a whole, with the result that it yields to the listener the full benefit of its teaching.

2. Does Not Explain the Story

If the story itself has not already explained itself, when it reaches the climax, then it is too late to explain the story in an ending. If the story is good in its form, and is properly told, the listener will get the right impression, whatever his age, without any explanation of any kind in the ending, and, if he does not get it from the story itself, it is certain that he will not get it from any amount of explaining. Moreover, the listener resents being regarded as an ignoramus.

The "tacked on moral," therefore, is inadvisable. A certain story-teller sadly blunders when he ends a story of the death of Thomas Hovenden with: " Such a picture of unselfishness, heroism, and Christlike abandon to save a child, is a picture to be admired in heaven—a picture worthy to hang in a palace."

Now, if this story really does teach heroism, then the listener already has this idea, long before the story-teller can get to his superfluous " preachiness."

3. Adds Nothing to the Story

The ending must not contain any addition to the story, any new event or any new idea, because anything new in the ending will serve as a distraction, and interfere seriously with the impression of the story. In other words, it is not the province of the ending of the story to *say anything,* but only to bring to a close that which already has been said in the story itself.

4. Measurably Satisfies Curiosity

In the climax, the story is brought to a point, something has turned out, and curiosity is measurably satisfied, with the result that the listener now may view the story as a completed whole, and may gain its full teaching.

And this is absolutely necessary to the success of the story, for, so long as curiosity is unsatisfied, the attention is directed forward and not backward, and the listener is expecting something more to come, instead of looking at and appreciating that which already has come.

5. Is Consistent With the Story

The ending of the story must seem to be consistent with all that has preceded. Even in the climax, while the outcome may have been surprising, at the same time it was plausible, things might have reasonably turned out just that way, and now, in the ending, there must be no surprises of any kind, and certainly no contradictions, for this would serve as a distraction, and thus interfere with the desired impression.

6. May Consist of Words of the Hero

Frequently a story may appropriately end with direct discourse, and may consist of the words of the hero himself. When " The Runaway Pancake," for instance, has reached the climax with the wish of the pancake, as he is swallowed by the pig, that he had stayed at home to be eaten by the hungry children instead, the story might be made to end felicitously with the pancake saying, " But this is the end of me."

The occasional use of direct discourse, in an ending, will be promotive of variety and art and effectiveness, but probably, as a rule, the ending should be in indirect discourse, in the words of the story-teller.

7. May be Omitted Altogether

Sometimes, in a story for adults, particularly when the climax is of such a character as to cause the listener to laugh, the ending may be left off altogether. In this case, the ending will be inferred, or " understood," and no confusion will result. Usually, however, even for adults, the story might better have an ending.

READING AND DISCUSSION

1. Analyze some familiar story, naming and numbering its events.

2. Select five stories, and write out a new beginning for each.

3. Write a new ending also for each of these five stories.

4. Select some one story, and write for it five different beginnings.

5. Write for this same story five different endings.

6. Read and criticize Chapter II in St. John's " Stories and Story-Telling."

CHAPTER VI

DEFINITION OF THE STORY

The story is a narrative of actual or imaginary events, so arranged as to constitute a vitally related whole, making a single definite impression, and so told as to bring about a change for the better in the listener.

1. The Story as a Form of Narrative

The story is narration in a specialized form. Narration has been defined as follows: " Narration is the recounting, in succession, of the particulars that make up a transaction." In general, two kinds of narration may be distinguished, namely, history and fiction.

(1) Relation of the Story to History

History may be defined as the systematic recounting of actual events that are considered important in the progress of the human race. One type of story, namely, the history-story, is history in the sense that it is a narrative of actual events.

History, however, includes much that the history-story cannot use, while, on the other hand, the history-story makes important use of a wide range of material which is not considered to be of sufficient importance to justify a place in history.

The best part of history is biography, which is the narration of actual events in the life of an individual. Biography provides much valuable material for history-stories, but there are many good history-stories which draw their material from individuals whose biographies are not written. The story of even a modest present-day hero or heroine may be far more effective, under given circumstances, than any story that can be drawn from the books of biography.

The trained story-teller does not make a fetish of history. He does, of course, draw freely from the books of history and biography, but, at the same time, he realizes that his best stories are ever in the process of making, in the lives of his fellow-beings about him, only awaiting the touch of the magic of his dramatic art. Indeed, the story-teller's best stories will come out of his own life.

(2) Relation of the Story to Fiction

Fiction, which is invented narrative, or the narration of imaginary events, is akin to legend-stories, parable-stories, fable-stories, myth-stories, fairy-stories, and allegory-stories, in that it does not confine itself to literal facts, but there are important differences.

The *novel,* one type of fiction, is much longer than the story, is more complex in plot, and may or may not teach truth, whereas the story seeks always primarily to teach and only incidentally to entertain.

The *short story,* another type of fiction, while shorter than the novel usually, in actual length, is, as a rule, much longer than the story. The short story, like the novel, seeks chiefly to entertain, but, unlike the novel and like the story, it seeks to make a single impression.

The *drama* is a type of fiction " wherein the characters speak for themselves, making as it were the story before our eyes." The story is like the drama in that it is dramatic in form and in that it allows the characters to make the story themselves, but it is shorter than the drama, and far simpler in construction. Moreover, it differs from the drama in that it has a more serious purpose, as a rule.

2. All Real Stories Are True

If a story is not true, it is not a story. It may not be literally true, but it must be essentially true. The truth of the story is not dependent on actual facts, but on essential truth. The world is full of facts which are not truths. Facts are important only as they are related to truth, to impression, to life.

(1) Literalness Not Essential

If the story does, incidentally, make use of facts, that is, if its events are actual events, then they are important because these actual events are so arranged as to constitute a vitally related whole, making a single definite impression, and so told as to bring about a change for the better in the listener.

On the other hand, the events of the story may be imaginary events, but they seem real, just as real as actual events, and, because they are skilfully arranged and dramatically handled, they make a true impression and bring about a change for the better in the listener. Therefore, this narrative of imaginary events is a true story. It is a misuse of the word true to say of any story that it is not true. All stories that teach truth are true, and the literalness or non-literalness of the events is wholly unimportant.

(2) Reality is Essential

The events in the story may not have occurred literally, actually, at any particular time, in any definite place, and may be the result of the skilful exercise of the constructive imagination, but such narrative of imaginary events, setting forth essential reality, teaches truth just as effectively as would a narrative of actual events, provided, of course, there is not made a false formal claim for its literalness. To definitely affirm that the imaginary events of a story actually occurred is lying.

Two terms have been used in connection with storytelling which would seem to be quite misleading, namely, *realistic* and *idealistic*. When the story is a narrative of actual events, it is called realistic; and, when it is a narrative of imaginary events, it is called idealistic. As a matter of fact, the events in all stories seem real and are essentially realistic. So, likewise, all stories present ideals, and are essentially idealistic.

3. Makes a Single Definite Impression

If a story teaches two things, it does not teach anything. One story teaches only one thing, and must teach only one thing in order to teach anything. Indeed, no single story attempts to teach even one whole virtue or a complete quality of character, but rather to teach one phase of one virtue, one quality of character, or one type of conduct.

(1) Limited in Scope

In teaching honesty, for instance, many stories are required to develop in the life the attitude and appreciation and practice of honesty. One story will teach a reward of honesty, a second will teach a penalty of dishonesty, a third will teach a duty in honesty, a fourth will teach a satisfaction in being honest, and so on almost indefinitely.

Take selfishness as another example. The story of the boy who could not get his hand out of the jar of nuts until he let go of some of the nuts teaches that it does not pay to be greedy, while the story of the dog in the manger teaches that selfishness is unreasonable. So there are other stories to teach many other phases of this virtue.

(2) Moral and Climax

In every case, the story makes known some one phase of truth, making right desirable and wrong undesirable, and tends to develop better life and conduct. And this single definite impression is made when the listener gets the point of the story, the lesson, the moral, the teaching.

The impression is made as soon as the story reaches a climax. The climax " is that which makes the story." Without it there is no story—only an accumulation of words. Everything in the story must lead up to and help to make the climax. The climax is the load in the gun. As soon as the climax is reached, the story must stop with a brief sentence or two of ending. The story itself is done.

4. A Change for the Better in the Listener

The real story has a very serious and a very practical purpose. Incidentally it entertains and instructs, but its chief concern is to bring about a change for the better in the life and conduct of the listener. Every story, then, is a teaching-story, a character-story, and achieves its aim vitally, dramatically, practically, effectively.

(1) Story-telling and Exposition

Story-telling may be distinguished from *exposition.* "Exposition is invention dealing with ideas or generalizations," whereas the story deals with characters, events, particulars, and therefore makes a stronger appeal to the imagination, the emotions, and the will. In other words, the story goes far beyond instruction, which is the aim of exposition, and includes reformation.

Six types of exposition are distinguished by the rhetorician, namely, (1) *definition,* which classifies an object, (2) *exegesis,* which amplifies definition, (3) *antithesis,* which emphasizes by contrast, (4) *iteration,* which repeats the same idea in different form, (5) *example,* which gives in the concrete the meaning of the abstract, and (6) *analogy,* which indicates likenesses.

All of these have their place, of course, in teaching, but the story is more effective than any one of them, and indeed than all of them together. Take *example,* for instance. To say that a certain individual gave one-fifth of his total income to religion and charity, is an example of liberality, and is effective, but, to tell the story of this individual's liberality, to show his liberality in action, dramatically, is far more effective. Most of our so-called "illustrations" consist of examples and analogies, and, while they are valuable, they are not stories.

(2) Story-telling and Argumentation

Story-telling also may be distinguished from *argumentation.* "Argumentation is invention dealing with truths, either ideas or facts." Argumentation differs from exposition in that it is concerned with the testing of the truth of things. The story is concerned with truths, but only with vital truths in their practical relations. Moreover, *the story does not argue for the truth, but rather assumes that it is true,* and thus depends on indirect suggestion, which is far more effective than the direct suggestion of argumentation.

In other words, in contrast with argumentation, the story is concerned only incidentally with truth as truth, in itself, but chiefly with the power of truth, with making truth effective in the life. Argumentation is at its best when it is persuasion, and persuasion is at its best when it is story.

The story does what all good teaching must do, and does it most effectively. It accomplishes its purpose through the threefold appeal to the whole being. First, through the appeal to the imagination and other intellectual functions, it makes truth *real,* and thus enables the listener to *know* it. Second, through the appeal to the emotions, it makes truth *attractive,* and thus enables the listener to *want* it. Third, through the appeal to the will, it makes the truth *effective,* and thus enables the listener to *do* it. In brief, the story promotes attitudes of mind, develops qualities of character, and suggests modes of behavior.

5. Example of a True Story

There has grown out of my own experience a story that is a narrative of imaginary events, and which I have told to various groups of boys and girls about nine, ten, and eleven years of age, with most gratifying results.

I should not allow anyone to say of this story that it is not true. The boys and girls themselves never have raised the question of its literalness or non-literalness, for the reason that they are too busy with its essential truth.

When Roger started to school, one morning, he said, " Good-bye, mamma." His mother said, " Good-bye, son. Be a good boy today." He said, " Yes'm." On the way to school he had a quarrel with another boy, and they got into a fight. At noon they had another fight, and, on the way home, still another fight.

He had three fights in one day, and he had not intended to have any fights. He had meant it when he said " Yes'm " to his mother. When he reached home, and told his mother about it, she said, " You promised mamma to be a good boy." " I know I did," said Roger, " but I could not help it. Robert called me a bad name, and I just biffed him one before I thought."

Another day, when Roger had disobeyed his mother, he said, " I don't know why it is that I just will be bad, sometimes. There seems to be something inside of me that makes me bad." His mother said, " That is exactly the trouble. It is ' out of the heart ' that the bad things come."

" Well," said Roger, " I just can't help it, then, and I am not to blame." Said his mother, " Let us see who is to blame." So, drawing Roger to her side, she talked to him about the bad in his heart, and about who was to blame. She told him that she was partly to blame, that his father was partly to blame, that his older brother was partly to blame, that his younger sister was partly to blame. " But there is one other to blame," she said, "and that is Roger. And Roger must try to get and keep these bad things out of his heart."

"All right," said Roger, "you take them out." "I cannot do that," said his mother. "If I had been able to do that I should have taken them out long ago."

Then, one day, Roger said to the minister, "Pastor, please get the bad things out of my heart, so I can be a good boy." "I do not know how to do that, my boy," said the minister. "I wish I did." "Then I want to be baptized," said Roger. "Why do you want to be baptized?" asked the minister. "So I can get the bad things out of my heart," answered Roger. "It is a good thing to be baptized, but the water cannot get into your heart and make it clean," said the minister.

"Then I want to join the church," said Roger. "It is a fine thing to belong to the church, and everyone ought to be a church-member, but the church has no heart-mop with which to clean out your heart," said the minister. "There is only One who can get the bad things out of your heart, Roger, and keep it clean." And the minister told Roger about that One.

One Sunday, while Roger was listening to the sermon, he heard a knock at the door of his heart, and a voice saying, "Open the door of your heart, and let me come in, and I will get the bad things out of your heart, and keep it clean." Again, one Sunday, during Sunday school, Roger heard that knock, knock, knock, and the same kind voice—"Open the door of your heart, and let me come in."

Then, one night, after Roger had gone to bed, and was trying to go to sleep, he said, "I wish I were not such a bad boy. I wish I could get all the bad things out of my heart, and keep them out. I wish I could be a good Christian." Just then he heard again that knock, knock, knock at the door of his heart, and the same gentle voice saying, " Open the door of your heart, and let me come in." And Roger said, " Come in! Come in! "

And He came in.

READING AND DISCUSSION

1. Discuss the story of Roger's heart. Is it a true story? Why?

2. See the following: Partridge, pages 7, 17, 22, 29, 117-120; Forbush, Chapter XIX; St. John, Chapters I and XII; Wyche, Chapter I; Keyes, page 34; Cather, Chapters I and XIII.

3. Name the story which has most influenced your life, and seek to explain its power.

4. Practice telling stories, and court criticism.

CHAPTER VII

TYPES OF STORIES

Stories may be classified, according to literary type, as follows: History-stories, legend-stories, parable-stories, fable-stories, myth-stories, fairy-stories, allegory-stories. Every teaching-story should fall into one of these seven classes.

1. HISTORY-STORIES

Definition: *History-stories teach truth through the selective presentation of actual occurrences in human lives.*

In this definition, the word *history* is used in a limited sense. Originally, the word meant *something learned by inquiry,* and it has come to mean, popularly, a *systematic record of actual occurrences in the lives of human beings that are considered important for the understanding of nations,* whereas the history-story is such a selection of actual occurrences as are considered *important in the teaching of the truth,* that is, in the bringing about of a change for the better in the listener or group of listeners.

The interest of history is focused upon those *of whom* it tells, while that of the history-story is focused upon those *to whom* it tells; history looks *backward,* while the history-story looks *forward;* history *explains* the past, while the history-story *makes* the present and the future; history *reveals* what has been achieved, while the history-story *creates* that which does not yet exist.

66

In considering these distinctions between history and the history-story, it should be recognized that history, through a continuous process of revision and readjustment, for a generation or more, has been gradually approaching the view-point of the history-story, and this change has made history more interesting and more helpful.

The history-story has four chief sources, namely, history, biography, current literature, and personal experience. From these four sources, the history-story draws freely and impartially, on the basis of selection for the teaching of truth. Frequently it happens that the most obscure characters furnish the most important events.

2. LEGEND-STORIES

Definition: *Legend-stories teach truth through the narration of imaginary events which attribute to well-known human beings actions in harmony with their known character.*

The word legend, in its derivation, means simply *something read,* and, popularly, it is used quite loosely. Legend, in the sense in which it is here used, is true, because it teaches truth, but it is not literally true.

Usually the legend is attached to some well-known historical character, and grows out of popular interest in the individual or out of admiration for him. Frequently it reveals the true character of the individual, and, in any event, it makes a true impression upon the listener, bringing about a change for the better.

Frequently, it is exceedingly *difficult to draw accurately the line between history-story and legend-story,* for the reason that there may be no way of determining definitely whether or not all the events actually occurred. Probably examples of legend-stories are " George Washington and the Cherry Tree," " Abraham Lincoln and the Pig," " St. Patrick and the Snakes," and " What Pershing said to the German Peace-Ambassadors."

3. PARABLE-STORIES

Definition : *Parable-stories teach truth through imaginary events which are within the range of ordinary experience and observation.*

Parable, in its etymology, means *something thrown alongside,* and popularly, the term is used quite loosely, chiefly of certain stories in the Bible. Some Bible stories which are called parables are not parable-stories at all, and the larger number of parables are outside the Bible. In fact, the largest number of modern stories are of this type.

The parable-story does not have in mind any particular individual or individuals, but it seems real, and is probable or possible in any ordinary human experience. It is not literally true, but it is essentially true, because it teaches truth.

Frequently, in reading a story, or in hearing it told, *one cannot know whether it is history-story or parable-story until he learns the history of its origin,* and, in that case, unless he knows that it is a history-story, he may classify it as a parable-story.

So far as the parable-story itself is concerned, it never raises the question of literalness or non-literalness. It simply assumes that the events are actual, without making any formal claims, and moves right along exactly as if they were. Thus it succeeds in creating the illusion of reality, and in making its true impression. It is a true story.

Indeed, it is *exceedingly difficult sometimes to determine whether it is history-story or parable-story, even when you are in full possession of all the facts connected with the origin of the story.* The history-story, as well as the parable-story, requires, in its making, such a selection and arrangement of events as will clothe it with the dramatic qualities of effectiveness, and it is exceedingly difficult, at times, to determine when a selection and arrangement of events may become practically a creating of events.

Sometimes also the memory is at fault. Unless short-hand notes are taken at the time, it is not humanly possible always to retain and reproduce accurately and literally, while, at other times, it is not advisable to do so, for the reason that a dramatic editing will make for effectiveness.

In some cases, a history-story will pass through a process of unconscious revision that will cause it gradually to become a parable-story, and which at the same time will make it the more effective. Perhaps we shall have to place here some of the stories of the popular evangelist. On the other hand, probably we ought to say, in justice to the evangelist, in this connection, that the story which is presented as history-story, and which we may have heard related before as personal experience of other individuals, may be literally true, in fact, for the reason that it may have been an actual experience common to several individuals.

4. FABLE-STORIES

Definition: *Fable-stories teach truth through the narration of imaginary events which attribute human characteristics to the lower animals and to the forces and objects of nature.*

Fable means *something spoken,* but any type of story is of course something spoken. Many stories found in collections of " Fables " really are not fables at all, according to our definition.

The fundamental reason for attributing human characteristics to the lower animals, and to the forces and objects of nature, and the explanation of the success of the fable-story, is that the characters thus become more real to the listener, and this illusion of reality makes for effectiveness in the teaching of the truth which it contains. Sometimes also this attribution of human characteristics makes the truth of the story more palatable, so to speak, by reason of its indirectness, and its appeal to the sense of humor.

Some of the well-known fable-stories are the following: " The Fox and the Cat," " The Fox and the Grapes," " The Dog in the Manger," " The Boys and the Frogs," and the " Bre'r Rabbit " stories.

5. MYTH-STORIES

Definition: *Myth-stories teach truth through the narration of imaginary events which express traditional beliefs and explanations with reference to the forces and objects of nature and the lower animals.*

Etymologically, myth means *something said*, but any story is something said. The myth-story is closely related to the legend-story, but the latter has to do with persons, while the former has to do with nature.

The value of the myth-story today usually is dependent on our ability to make it teach something different from its original teaching, and is, therefore, the most difficult to handle of all the types of stories.

Some of the well-known myth-stories are the following: "Why the Robin's Breast is Red," "The Man in the Moon," "Prometheus, the Greek Fire-Giver," "The Story of the Sunflower," "How the Camel Got His Hump," "Thor and Thunder."

6. FAIRY-STORIES

Definition: *Fairy-stories teach truth through the narration of strange or supernatural events, frequently involving sudden changes in size and location.*

Etymologically, fairy means *enchantment,* and this meaning hints at present usage. The fairy-story is likely to have in it fairies, sprites, elfs, goblins, dwarfs, etc.

Many fairy-stories are *folk-tales,* having originated early in the development of a race of people, and having been told for many generations before they were put into written form. Other types of stories also are to be classed as folk-tales, namely, myth-stories, some fable-stories, some parable-stories, some legend-stories, and some allegory-stories.

Among the well-known fairy-stories are "The Golden Goose," "Diamonds and Toads," "The Frog King," "The Sleeping Beauty," "Jack and the Beanstalk,"

" Jack the Giant Killer," " Aladdin and His Wonderful Lamp," " Boots and His Brothers."

7. ALLEGORY-STORIES

Definition: *Allegory-stories teach truth through the narration of imaginary events which, in their form, indicate hidden meanings in ordinary events and characteristics.*

Allegory means, in its derivation, *haranguing another,* and this meaning does not enter into our definition. This type of story is the most artificial, and the most difficult of construction, but it is true, because it teaches truth.

An example of a modern allegory-story is the author's " Mr. Sunday School and the Doctor."

Mr. Sunday School was sick.

His wife said to him, " I wish you would let me call in Doctor Specialist. He cured Uncle Sermon and Aunt Music, and our neighbors, Mr. Business and Mrs. Public School, and I am sure he could cure you."

" No, I'm not going to have any doctor. Doctors cost money, and, besides, if I call in a doctor, everybody will know I'm sick, and I don't want anybody to know it. I know what's the matter with me, and I can cure myself. I'm suffering from Irregularity." So he took some of Doctors Cross and Crown Tablets, but grew no better.

His wife came to him again, and said, " I wish you'd let me call in Doctor Specialist. I just know he could cure you." " No, I'm not going to have any doctor, I tell you. I can cure myself. I'm suffering from Tardiness." So he took some of Doctor Scold's Liniment;

but he took it internally instead of externally, and it almost killed him.

His wife said again, "Do let me call in the doctor. I just hate to see you suffer so." "How many times do I have to tell you I'm not going to have any old doctor? The only thing that's the matter with me is Non-Preparation, and I can cure myself." So he tried some of Doctor Exhortation's Tea—drank gallons of it—but could note no improvement in the way he felt.

Again Mrs. Sunday School said, "Husband, dear, I wish you'd let me call Doctor Specialist." "I tell you I'm not going to have any doctor. I'm going to cure myself. I'm suffering from Confusion." So he took some of Doctor Bell's and Doctor Yell's Stimulant, and became almost a raving maniac.

His wife came to him in tears, "Sunday, dear, I can't bear to see you suffer so. *Please* let me call the doctor." "I *will not* have the doctor. That's final! The only thing that's the matter with me is Worldliness, and I can cure myself." So he took some of Dr. Pious Talk's Pink Pills, but could note no improvement.

Mrs. Sunday School said, "Aren't you going to let me call Doctor Specialist, dear?" "Don't mention that doctor to me again. I'm going to cure myself. I'm suffering from Diminution." So he tried some of Doctor Contest's Electric Treatments. As long as he kept up the treatments he took on flesh, but, as soon as he stopped, he lost all he had gained, and grew steadily worse.

Then his wife said, "I don't care what you say, I'm going to call Doctor Specialist. I'm tired of having a sick man around the house." So she went to the telephone and said, "Hello, Central, give me Efficiency 1921.

Hello, is this Doctor Specialist? This is Mrs. Sunday
School. Mr. Sunday School is sick, and I want you to
come over and see him right away. What? Oh, at the
corner of Mossback Avenue and Conservative Boule-
vard. All right. Good-bye."

Doctor Specialist came, examined the patient, diag-
nosed the case, and pronounced it a severe attack of
Ignoramusitis. He prescribed a reorganization cathartic,
a teacher-training tonic, a graded-lesson diet, departmental exercises, and divine companionship.

Mrs. Sunday School saw to it that her husband took
the medicine regularly and followed the doctor's instruc-
tions faithfully, and five years from that time he was the
healthiest man in the state of Improvement.

And his wife said, " I told you Doctor Specialist could
cure you."

READING AND DISCUSSION

1. Memorize and justify the seven definitions given in
this chapter.

2. Classify five stories not named in this chapter.

3. Is a speaker ever justified in saying, " Please pardon
a personal illustration "? Why?

4. Note, in " A Manual of Stories," by Forbush,
Chapter III and Appendix I, that the classifications
are popular, and not scientific.

5. Note, in Sly's " World Stories Retold," another
loose, popular classification, as follows: (1) " Bible
Stories." Classification on the basis of source. There
are various literary types of stories in the Bible. (2)
" Missionary Stories." Again the source is the basis of

classification. (3) "Play Stories." Classification on the basis of purpose. (4) "Fairy and Folk-Tales." Many folk-tales are not fairy-stories, and some of them are. (5) "Fables." Many stories here indicated are not fable-stories at all. (6) "Myths." Classification on the basis of literary type. (7) "Legends." Classification on the basis of literary type. (8) "Nature-Stories." Classification on the basis of source. (9) "Allegorical-Stories." Classification on the basis of literary type. (10) "Historical-Stories." Classification on the basis of literary type. (11) "Biographical-Stories." Literary type. (12) "Altruistic-Stories." Purpose. (13) "Love-Stories." Purpose. (14) "Vocational Stories." Purpose. (15) "Instructional Stories." Purpose. But that is the purpose of all stories, using the word instruction in the vital sense. (16) "Humorous Stories." Puts the emphasis upon a quality in the story, and one that is quite incidental.

6. Other examples of loose classification of stories are to be found in "Story-Telling for Upper Grade Teachers," by Cross and Statler, Chapter III, and in "Stories and Story-Telling," by St. John, Chapter XIII.

7. Note, in "Story-Telling in School and Home," by Partridge, Chapters V to X inclusive, an approach to a scientific classification, but one that is still largely of the popular character. Chapter XIII is entitled "Educational Story-Telling." All story-telling is educational, if we use the term education in its broad and vital sense. Chapter XVII is entitled "The Story in Moral Education." Every real story, when psychologically analyzed, will be found to be usable in moral education.

CHAPTER VIII

GRADING OF STORIES

" I don't like that story," said one of my students,
when asked to tell a certain story before a class, for
criticism. " You have no right either to like or to dislike any story," I said. " It is the listeners who must like
it, and they only that they may give attention to it, and
may get and live its truth."

1. Necessity for Grading

" But, if I do not like the story," said the student, " can
I expect my listeners to like it?" " Certainly," I said.
" This story was made for individuals much younger than
yourself, and their interests and needs are very different
from yours. *The very qualities in the story which cause
you to dislike it may be exactly the ones which will
make it effective with those for whom it was intended.*"

" But," insisted the student, "how can I make myself
like the story if I do not like it?" " Why, that is not at
all impossible," I said. " First, let us determine, in the
light of the best conclusions of genetic psychology, just
where this story belongs. Then imagine yourself to be
in that period of life, with its particular interests and
needs, and soon the story will take on a new interest,
and you will come to like it because you will see that it is
a good story, and that *it will be effective with its proper
audience.*"

After some further discussion, we decided on the

story's grading, and the student adopted the suggestions which had been given, and was able to come into a proper appreciation of the story under consideration.

During the discussion, one of the members of the class said, "Do you not think that a good story is good for everybody?" "No," I said, "it is not. *However good a story may be, it is good for only a limited constituency,* those individuals into whose interests it fits definitely and whose particular needs it meets effectively."

"But," said another, "do you not think that some stories are universal in their appeal?" "No," I said, "*there is no story with a universal appeal.* It may be true that some stories have a wider range of appeal than do others, but it is a limited range at the best. Stories must be graded just as all teaching materials must be graded."

"But," opposed still another, "I think there are some children's stories, for instance, that are interesting to adults, and some adult stories that are interesting to children." "There would seem to be some ground for this opinion," I said, "if it were required only that the story be interesting, but it must be also, and chiefly, *effective*— that is, it must put its truth over into the life of the listener and bring about a change for the better."

"Do you mean," said the questioner, "that there are certain stories, for instance, which are distinctively and exclusively 'junior' stories?" "I do mean that exactly," I replied. "During the period usually called 'junior,' ages about nine to eleven inclusive, there are certain dominant interests and certain distinctive needs which make certain stories most effective in the life during this period."

"What is *the first question to ask,* then, in grading a story?" was one of the questions asked during this class discussion. "The first question always," I said, "in grading a story, is *'Will this story be interesting to the particular group in view?'* The story may be interesting, of course, and at the same time not be effective, but, nevertheless, it must be interesting in order to be effective. For, unless the story is interesting to the listener, he will not give attention to it, and, therefore, he will not get the impression, the teaching, the truth, the benefit. In order to be effective, the story must fit into the life of the listener, that is, it must be interesting to him, must have value for him, must satisfy a conscious need, must help him to solve his problem."

"Is it true," was asked, "that *each period of human life has its own particular story interests?*" "Undoubtedly," was the answer. "This change in interests from period to period is due to the ripening of instincts and the enlarging of experience. Interests are both innate, or immediate, and acquired, or mediate. The continuous changing in the interests of an individual is due, then, to two groups of influences, or stimuli, namely, inborn impulses from within and suggestions from without. Of course, even the impulses from within are more and more acquired, and less and less innate, as the experience enlarges."

"But," it was objected, "are there not certain interests that persist through life?" "There is a measure of truth there," was the reply, "in that probably no interest ever wholly disappears after it once appears, but at the same time each interest would appear to be strongest during a limited period immediately after its first appearance, and it is the interest at its best which must be considered in the grading of stories.

"Indeed, it would seem that *each period of life has some one new interest which is strongest during this period,* and that this interest is the dominant interest of the period. If this be true, then it is this dominant interest in each period that will constitute the story-teller's pole-star as he explores the domain of selection.

"Of course, always, it must be kept in mind that *there is considerable overlapping between the periods,* and that most of the interests continue to be effective after they once appear. Moreover, in addition to those interests peculiar to the various periods of life and common to all normal human beings, there are *certain other special interests* to be considered, such as those which are due to vocation and avocation. 'Shop talk' always is interesting even in a story. A farm story, for instance, is more interesting to farmers than to those who dwell in a city and who know little of rural life."

2. Basis for Grading

With this discussion of interests in mind, we are now in a position to arrive at a scientific basis for the proper grading of stories. In the grading of stories, we should keep in mind the *materials* of which the story is composed, the *form* in which the materials are presented, and the *teaching* of the events.

(1) Materials

The materials of the story must, in themselves, make essential connection with the dominant story-interests of the listener. For the first period of the student's life, the story will deal particularly with *things;* for the second period, with *individuals* as such; for the third period, with *relations* of individuals to others; for the fourth period, with *activities;* for the fifth period, with *ideas* and ideals; for the sixth period, with *vocations* and avocations; for the seventh period, with relations between the *sexes;* for the eighth period, with the great *problems* of life.

The materials of which the story is composed must have chief consideration in all grading. A story, for instance, composed of materials having to do with relations between the sexes, might possess all the excellencies as to its form and teaching, and might be " heavenly " to an eighteen-year-old, but to a ten-year-old, it would be " Mush! "

(2) Form

The literary form, or type, of the story must have important consideration in grading, for the reason that some forms better adapt themselves to some periods than to others. At the same time, it must be kept in mind that some types have a range of suitability covering several periods.

History-stories, which teach truth through the selective presentation of actual occurrences in human lives, are better suited to the *later periods,* as a rule, than to the earlier periods, but at the same time it must be kept in mind that there are history-stories for all ages.

Legend-stories, which teach truth through the narration of imaginary events which attribute to well-known human beings actions in harmony with their known character, are most suitable, usually, for ages about *twelve to fourteen,* chiefly for the reason that their materials are mainly all idealistic, but there are some legends suitable for later periods.

Parable-stories, which teach truth through imaginary events which are within the range of ordinary experience and observation, adapt themselves to the materials for *all the periods* of life. Indeed, the parable-story is the most universal of all the types, the history-story coming next in its universality.

Fable-stories, which teach truth through the narration of imaginary events which attribute human characteristics to the lower animals, usually adapt themselves best to the materials suitable for the years about *four to eight,* but there would seem to be no reason why we should not use fable-stories effectively also for all the later periods, if we could find somebody to write them. Most of the fable-stories which we have are folk-tales, and their brevity, simplicity, and naiyetè would seem to justify our placing of them in the earlier period.

Myth-stories, which teach truth through the narration of imaginary events which express traditional beliefs and explanations with reference to the forces and objects of nature, adapt themselves chiefly to the materials which are suitable for the ages about *four to eight,* along with the fable-stories, and for similar reasons.

Fairy-stories, which teach truth through the narration of strange or supernatural events, and frequently involving sudden changes in size and location, are suitable chiefly for the ages about *four to eight,* along with the fable-stories and myth-stories, and for similar reasons. We have, however, some good fairy-stories for the later periods, and we ought to have more.

Allegory-stories, which teach truth through the narration of imaginary events which, in their form, indicate hidden meanings in ordinary events and characteristics, are suitable chiefly for *young people and adults* and not at all for the earlier periods, for the reason that they involve considerable experience in abstract reasoning.

(3) Teaching

Preliminary to the grading of a story, always it is important to ask the question, " Just what does this story teach? " The answer to this question, taken in connection with the materials and the form, will assist in the proper placing of the story.

It would seem that *there are, in each of the life periods, certain attitudes, qualities of character, and modes of behavior which need especially to be taught at this particular time.* Stories that teach obedience to parents, for instance, will come early in life, while those that teach against neglect or mistreatment of parents will come in the later periods. That familiar fairy-story, " The Runaway Pancake," one of the most popular of old folk-tales, teaches a lesson in obedience—that it does not pay to run away from home—and belongs therefore to the earliest period, when the child, at about three years of age, is likely to run away from the house and into danger.

3. Dominant Story Interests

An outline of what would seem to be the dominant story interests of life, with brief discussion, may serve as an approximate guide in dealing with the materials of the story. It must be understood that this outline is not offered as a complete statement.

(1) Things

In the first story-telling period, during infancy, ages about two and three, known as the cradle-roll period in the Sunday school, the dominant story interest may be best indicated by the term *things.*

This is the *sense* period, when these small human beings are interested chiefly in experiencing sensations over and over again, that they may get better and better acquainted with things. More and more, their sensations are yielding perceptions, and they are beginning to acquire various concepts as the building materials of the mental life.

They are interested chiefly therefore in the common objects of nature, in ordinary household objects, in simple rhythmical repetitions, in little rhymes and jingles, in parts of their own body, etc., etc.

(2) Individuals

In the second period, during early childhood, ages about four and five, known as the beginners, or kindergarten, period in the Sunday school, the dominant story interest may be indicated by the term *individuals.* Children of this age are able now to appreciate self as an individual, and also others as individuals—parent, brother or sister, playmate, domestic animal, insect, bird, etc., etc.

(3) Groups

In the third period, during middle childhood, ages about six to eight, grades one to three in the public school, known as the primary period in the Sunday school, the dominant story interest may be indicated by the term *groups.*

In this period, the social instincts are ripening, and the children are coming now to have relations with a larger number of individuals, so they are interested not only in individuals as individuals, but also in the relations of individuals to individuals. They are interested therefore in stories which depict various home and school activities, which picture individuals playing with other individuals.

(4) Achievement

In the fourth period, during later childhood, ages about nine to eleven, grades four to six in the public school, known as the junior period in the Sunday school, the dominant story interest may be indicated by the term *achievement*.

In this period, the growing experiences of the children enable them to distinguish more accurately between fact and fancy, and better to coordinate mind and muscle. It is a period of slow growth and good health, and their lives are characterized by much activity. Therefore, they are interested in stories whose materials are composed chiefly of doing, deeds, achievement.

(5) Attainment

In the fifth period, during early adolescence, ages about twelve to fourteen, grades seven to nine, or junior high school, known as the intermediate period in the Sunday school, the dominant story interest may be indicated by the term *attainment*.

In this period, the enlarged experience enables these young adolescents better to discern the character of the doer behind the doing, and to form ideals.

(6) Vocations

In the sixth period, during middle adolescence, ages about fifteen to seventeen, grades ten to twelve, or senior high school, known as the senior period in the Sunday school, the dominant story interest may be indicated by the term *vocations*.

In this period, these developing adolescents feel that they are getting to be men and women, and that they must find their place in life. They are seeking to find themselves and to place themselves in the world, and they are interested, therefore, in stories which involve the vocational interests.

(7) Courtship

In the seventh period, during later adolescence, or youth, ages about eighteen to twenty-four, college and university, known as the young people's period in the Sunday school, the dominant story interest may be indicated by the term *courtship*.

In this period, the sexual impulse is strong, and it colors the whole life, which is characterized, therefore, by dreams and plans of home-making.

(8) Struggle

In the eighth period, during adulthood, about twenty-five and over, the dominant story interest may be. indicated by the term *struggle*. Life now is serious and full of a variety of problems. Courtship and struggle in stories for this period make a powerful combination.

Particularly suitable, in this period, are stories of struggle and achievement drawn from the varied experiences of contemporary life, as well as the biographies of the great men and women of history.

READING AND DISCUSSION

1. For the names and sources of many stories, with suggestions as to their grading, see " A List of Character-Building Stories," pages 263 to 277, in " A Manual of Stories," by Forbush.

2. For a comprehensive graded list of stories, see pages 270 to 296, in " Story-Telling for Upper Grade Teachers," by Cross and Statler.

3. Select five stories for grading, indicating where they belong, and giving your reasons.

CHAPTER IX

TESTING AND STUDYING STORIES

There are two individuals involved in the telling of a story, namely, the story-teller and the listener, and the success of the story-teller is determined by the reaction, or response, of the listener. And there is likely to be a more satisfactory response if the story-teller will make it a practice carefully to study his stories before telling them.

TESTING THE STORY

1. Story-telling Must Give Pleasure

Generally speaking, in order to be effective, story-telling must be liked, enjoyed. The youngest listener will say, " Tell it again." One a little older will say, " Tell another story." One still older may join with others in hand-clapping.

During the telling of a story, the listener will indicate his interest by an attitude of attention. He will be looking at the story-teller, unconsciously imitating his facial expressions, and nodding or shaking the head. There will be a lighting up of the face, laughing, crying, leaning forward, sitting still, etc., according to the age of the listener and the nature of the story.

On the other hand, it should be said that the mere fact that the listener liked the story is not evidence of the success of the story, for his pleasure may have been due to the form of the story or to excellence in its telling rather than to its teaching value for him.

Also it is true that a story may be effective, and that it may be enjoyed as a whole, and at the same time evoke unpleasant feelings. It may evoke the emotion of fear, it may arouse concern for a story-character, and it may cause him to " feel bad " because of something he has done.

2. Story-telling Must Evoke Thought

In listening to a good story, well told, the listener will perceive, imagine, remember, judge, and reason. He is not a mere spectator, but rather a participator. That is, he is *giving attention and is doing some purposive thinking*. The stream of consciousness is focused upon the story with favorable reactions.

Frequently, *the listener identifies himself with one of the individuals of the story*. Sometimes he will come to a very definite conclusion, and he may want to give expression to the same. He should be encouraged in this, and should be given helpful direction. He may desire to ask questions, after the story is done, and his questions should be heard and answered sympathetically and tactfully.

In some cases, after he has told a story, the storyteller may ask vital questions which will evoke real self-expression on the part of the listener, but any question designed to test the listener's memory with regard to some event in the story will serve to magnify the incidental and to minify the essential.

The youngest listeners cannot describe their mental processes or give expression to their emotions, and it is not wise to ask them questions, usually. If they appear interested during the telling of the story, you may be sure that they have been thinking. One way to test the thinking of the listener is through properly supervised handwork. On examination of the handwork, wrong impressions may be corrected.

3. Story-telling Must Develop Attitudes

Another test of story-telling is that it develops or strengthens right attitudes in the listener. It helps him into proper senses of values. It causes him to like and want the good, and to dislike and turn from the bad. It *develops in him an appreciation* of the good, the true, the noble, the better, the divine, the spiritual, the .beautiful, the uplifting.

Incidentally, good story-telling will tend to develop in the listener an appreciation of stories, but we must be on our guard, in dealing with children, against concluding that certain stories are good for them because they "like" them. Their liking of a story may be due to some type of action in it or to the fact that they have been taught to like it, and not because it is vitally helpful. We must give them such stories as will best develop in them the best attitudes and appreciations, giving but little consideration to any expressions of preference.

4. Story-telling Must Improve Behavior

Through the skilful presentation of true ideals of life and conduct, the listener is assisted in forming right ideals of conduct for himself, and in realizing these in his life. Some change for the better takes place in the listener, as in the case of the little girl who, after she has heard a story, said, " Mamma, I was a good Samaritan today."

There are *two ways of obtaining data with reference to changes in the listener's conduct,* namely, from the listener himself and from others about him. In the case of students in the elementary grades, there may be reports in class of week-day activities, and the parents may be induced to keep records and to make reports.

In the case of older students, reports from others sometimes are obtainable, and it is possible to get them to report on themselves, privately and in class. Occasionally it might be well to ask them to write out, in class, without signing their names, answers to such questions as the following: " Have your thinking and conduct been changed in any way by any story you have heard recently? Give name of story and indicate exactly in what way it has influenced you."

5. Story-telling May be Reproduced

After having heard the story, the listener may tell the story back to the story-teller and to others, may draw or mold a likeness of some object, individual, event, or impression of the story, may participate in a discussion of the purpose of the story, may tell another story suggested by the one he has just heard, or may assist in playing, or dramatizing, the story, according to age and circumstances.

In the dramatizing of stories the following suggestions may be kept in mind: (1) Let the students choose their own parts, with some tactful direction. (2) Let the students work out their own dramatization with a minimum of suggestion on the part of the teacher. (3)

Use costumes and scenery or not, according to place and circumstances, but usually it is better to let the imagination furnish these. (4) Train all students to speak distinctly and with proper modulation, and to impersonate freely. (5) After a dramatization, criticize sympathetically and constructively, and then repeat the dramatization, immediately or at a later time. (6) Outdoor dramatizations occasionally are practicable and advisable. (7) Almost any story may be profitably dramatized by students of almost any age.

Miss Elizabeth Erwin Miller, in her excellent book, " The Dramatization of Bible Stories," gives the following suggestive summary of the mode of procedure in developing a dramatization: "(1) Select a story with care; then adapt it for telling. (2) Tell the story, emphasizing the essential parts. (3) Let the children divide the story into pictures or scenes. (4) Have a discussion of what should take place in each scene. (5) Let volunteers from among the children act out one scene as they think it should be done, using their own words. (6) Develop criticism by the other children with suggestions for improvement. (7) Have a second acting of the scene for improvement. (8) Let each of the other scenes be worked out in the same manner. (9) See that every child has the chance to try out many parts. (10) Play the story through many times. Change it often according to the criticism, until the children recognize the result as a product of their best effort."

6. Story-telling May be Followed by Quiet

Sometimes it is well if the listener can be perfectly quiet for a moment after having heard a story, and, in the Sunday school, there might be a moment of silent prayer, followed by a sentence of uttered prayer or a stanza of an appropriate song. A group of students might be most helpfully dismissed with a story.

7. Story-telling Must be Trusted and Given Time

Probably the best results of story-telling can never be tabulated. The story does its work so subtly and unobtrusively as to make testing exceedingly difficult, and the story-teller must learn to trust the story and himself and the listeners.

If the story-teller has mastered the principles contained in this book, and is an alert and continuous student, and a faithful worker, he may rest assured that his story-telling will stand the test of time and eternity, and that it will produce the incomparable results of the one best method of teaching.

STUDYING THE STORY

Of course the listener will not analyze the story. He will only listen to it, and enjoy it, and image it, and feel it, and do it, without being conscious of its effect, and without knowing the why or the how of the process. But the story will fall short of its best effect unless the story-teller analyzes, criticizes, and organizes his materials.

1. Some Principles Involved

The story-teller should ask himself a number of questions about his story, in order that he may proceed with intelligence and conviction.

(1) What Grade?

In story-telling, as in all teaching, we begin with the student and not with the story. The story must fit into the interests and needs of the students, else it cannot be used, for the only reason for using the story at all is the student.

In the light of the principles set forth in Chapter VIII, combined with his knowledge of his students, the story-teller must determine whether or not the story under consideration is usable.

(2) What Teaching?

Definitely, just what does this story teach? If it does not teach anything, then it is not a story, and I cannot use it. Is this a true story, in the sense in which the story is defined in Chapter VI?

If so, then what is its teaching, its lesson, its moral, its truth? And just how may it be stated? It may be well to write out several possible statements, finally deciding on one word as indicating in general the teaching and then on a more full and complete statement.

(3) What Type?

This particular story must belong to one of the seven types as defined in Chapter VII, else that classification is not complete and scientific. A little practice will develop skill in classification on the part of the story-teller, and this will be a distinct aid to effectiveness.

Of course the determination of the grade, the teaching and the type of the story cannot be regarded as three successive steps, but rather as the three phases of a single process, for each is closely related to and is dependent on the other two.

(4) What Events?

What events are there in this story, and what may they be named? Where does the first event begin and end? So with the second event, and on through.

It will be well, indeed, for the story-teller's sole benefit, of course, to number and name the events, giving to each a concise, significant designation, in accordance with the principles discussed in Chapter V. Involved in this process, is the determination of the number of the events and their arrangement in effective order.

(5) What Beginning?

Has this story a good beginning? Why? Does it conform to the principles as enunciated in Chapter V? Will it accomplish its purpose? Is it brief enough? What of its contents and its form?

(6) What Ending?

Does the ending of this story conform to the principles set forth in Chapter V? Is it sufficiently brief? Does it explain or moralize? Does it add anything to the story? Does it measurably satisfy present curiosity?

(7) What Form?

Does the form of this story conform to the standard of Chapter IV? Does it measure up to the standard of action and movement? Does it employ familiar terms? Does it omit unnecessary words and phrases? Is it simple in its language constructions? Is there any place here for purposeful repetition? Is there sufficient definiteness?

Does it measure up to the standard of direct rather than indirect discourse? Does it make a strong appeal to the imagination, presenting the teaching as indirect suggestion, relieving the story-teller sufficiently of responsibility?

Does it measure up to the standard in the omission of all questions and in moving forward rapidly and smoothly?

(8) What Impersonation?

How may I best carry out, in this story, the suggestions of Chapter III? Just which character may I attempt to represent, and what characteristic may I imitate? What place is there here for the expression of emotion?

(9) What Gesture?

Just where, in this story, might gesture be particularly helpful, and what type of gesture would be suitable? How may I so use gesture as to conform to the principles as set forth in Chapter III?

(10) What Expression?

For what expressional activity on the part of the student would it be advisable to plan in connection with this story? After I shall have told the story, ought I to plan to ask questions or to encourage the student to ask questions?

Or ought I to plan for handwork of some kind that will deepen and test impression? Or ought I to plan for dramatization? Perhaps I shall decide to do both. It will depend on my group of students and my equipment, and on what expressional work we have had recently. I shall try to keep in mind the importance of varying the method of securing self-expression on the part of the students.

READING AND DISCUSSION

1. Make a careful study of at least ten good stories.

2. "Try out" a story on an individual or a group of individuals, making notes for yourself of any favorable or unfavorable reactions.

3. Listen to the conversation of a group of children after a story-telling period, and note any significant expressions.

4. Talk with the parents of children and make definite effort to discover some indications of the effects of story-telling.

5. Occasionally ask the listeners, if old enough, to write statements answering some such questions as follows: " What do you like best about this story, and why? Do you think this boy did right, and why? What would you have done if you had been in his place? "

CHAPTER X

CLASSIFYING STORIES

The student who would excel in story-telling should make a careful, detailed study of at least ten good stories, as suggested in the preceding chapter, with written analyses, until he is sure that he has mastered a method of applying the principles set forth in this book, and he should make for himself an ever-growing, annotated list of classified stories.

EXAMPLES OF ANALYZING

For purposes of illustration, as indicating a method of studying and analyzing, we may take two of the stories used in this book.

1. How Jane Learned to Tell Stories

The story in Chapter I of the student who felt that she never could learn to tell stories, but who did learn, may be analyzed as follows: (1) *Grade.* Best adapted to students from about sixteen to twenty-five years of age. (2) *Teaching.* Teaches story-telling—story-telling artistry may be acquired through a study of the principles and through practice. (3) *Type.* It is a history-story, the events being literally true. (4) *Events.* The events may be named as follows: First, her first attempt and failure; second, her second failure; third, her determination to quit trying; fourth, her gradual improvement;

fifth, her signal success. (5) *Beginning.* The beginning
is the first sentence. It is short, it indicates the leading
character, it names the place, and it suggests an atmosphere. It is simple and out of the ordinary, and likely
would get attention. (6) *Ending.* The ending is the last
sentence. It is short, it is in direct discourse, and it
leaves the conclusion to the listener. (7) *Form.* It is
simple in its language constructions, abounds in direct
discourse, and the action is rapid. This story would be
better if it were a little longer and took more time to
show more, and *told* less. (8) *Impersonation.* Impersonate the student, showing the discouragement in, " Oh,
I can't do it. I just can't tell a story." Show the different attitude in, " I can try it." Impersonate the other
students in the words of commendation, in the climax.
(9) *Gesture.* Indicate by gesture the reaching for the
newspaper clipping by the student, and the handing of it
to her by the teacher. Other places for gesture in the
story will suggest themselves. (10) *Expression.* This
is not the type of story that calls for handwork, or for
dramatization, but for class discussion.

2. Mr. Sunday School and the Doctor

This story, found in Chapter VII, may be analyzed
as follows: (1) *Grading.* It is best adapted to adults,
and to a special class of adults, namely, Sunday school
workers. (2) *Teaching.* It teaches religious education—
training for Sunday school work. (3) *Type.* It is a
modern allegory-story. (4) *Events.* The events may be
named as follows: First, wife recommends Doctor Specialist; second, Mr. Sunday School's first attempt to cure
himself; third, second attempt to cure himself; fourth,

third attempt to cure himself; fifth, fourth attempt to cure himself; sixth, fifth attempt to cure himself; seventh, sixth attempt to cure himself; eighth, the doctor's diagnosis and prescription; ninth, the cure. (5) *Beginning.* The beginning is " Mr. Sunday School was sick." The character is named, and both the place and an atmosphere are suggested. (6) *Ending.* The ending is the last sentence, in direct discourse. It is brief, and simply brings the story to a close, without any addition or distraction. (7) *Form.* The language constructions are simple, there is plenty of direct discourse, there are no unnecessary words or phrases, and the action is swift. (8) *Impersonation.* Impersonate both Mr. Sunday School and wife, all the way through, and also the doctor. (9) *Gesture.* Imitate the using of the telephone. Express Mr. Sunday School's pain and grouchiness. (10) *Expression.* This story has been dramatized, and also has been worked into a pageant.

SUGGESTIONS AS TO LISTS

No conscientious student of story-telling can afford to take at their face value the published lists of stories. He may accept these gratefully as suggestions, but should make his own card-file list. The list which follows is but briefly suggestive of a method of list-making.

1. Cradle Roll Period, Ages about Two and Three

(1) Appreciation

" The Golden Cobwebs," fairy-story, teaching interest in the Christmas tree. Telling-time, about four minutes. Found in " World Stories Retold."

(2) Helpfulness

" The Old Woman and Her Pig," fable-story, teaching that it pays to help others. Telling-time, about three minutes. Found in " For the Children's Hour."

(3) Kindness

" Baby Ray's Bedtime," fable-story, teaching that it pays to be kind to pets. Telling-time, about three minutes. Found in " For the Children's Hour."

(4) Meddlesomeness

" Goldilocks and the Three Bears," fable-story, teaching that it does not pay to meddle with the possessions of others. Telling-time, about three minutes. Found in " World Stories Retold."

(5) Obedience

" Raggylug," fable-story, teaching that it pays to mind mother. Telling-time, about three minutes. Found in " For the Children's Hour."

2. Beginners' Period, Ages about Four and Five

(1) Cleanliness

" The Pig Brother," fairy-story, teaching that it pays to be clean and neat. Telling-time, about five minutes. Found in " For the Children's Hour."

(2) Contentment

" The Runaway Pancake," fable-story, teaching that it does not pay to run away from home and duty. Telling-time, about three minutes. Found in "World Stories Retold."

"The Gingerbread Boy," fable-story, teaching that it does not pay to run away from home and duty. Telling-time, about five minutes. Found in "For the Children's Hour."

"Tale of the Littlest Mouse," fable-story, teaching that comfort in safety is better than luxury in fear. Telling-time, about ten minutes. Found in "For the Children's Hour."

(3) Credulity

"Why the Bear has a Stumpy Tail," fable-story, teaching that it does not pay to believe everything others say. Telling-time, about one minute. Found in "World Stories Retold."

3. Primary Period, Ages about Six to Eight

(1) Appreciation

"The Journey of a Drop of Water," fable-story, teaching that even a little drop of water has great value. Telling-time, about three minutes. Found in "Worth While Stories for Every Day."

(2) Avarice

"Midas and the Golden Touch," fairy-story, teaching that it does not pay to give money the first place in life. Telling-time, about five minutes. Found in "World Stories Retold."

(3) Cleanliness

"Tom, the Water Baby," fairy-story, teaching that untidiness makes one unattractive to others. Telling-time, about twelve minutes. Found in " For the Children's Hour."

4. Junior Period, Ages about Nine to Eleven

(1) Ambition

" The Log Cabin Boy, Abraham Lincoln," history-story, teaching that hard work makes dreams come true. Telling-time, about ten minutes. Found in "For the Children's Hour, Book Three."

(2) Christianity

" St. George and the Dragon," legend-story, teaching that the true Christian possesses the power that vanquishes evil. Telling-time, about seven minutes. Found in " World Stories Retold."

(3) Common Sense

" Foolish Fred," parable-story, teaching that those who do not use common sense likely will get into trouble. Telling-time, about four minutes. Found in " Worth While Stories for Every Day."

5. Intermediate Period, Ages about Twelve to Fourteen

(1) Filial Love

" The Girl Who Saved Her Father, Prascovia," history-story, teaching that true love for parents may involve heroic sacrifice. Telling-time, about twelve minutes. Found in " For the Children's Hour, Book Three."

(2) Friendship

"Damon and Pythias," legend-story, teaching that there is great power in unselfish friendship. Telling-time, about three minutes. Found in " Worth While Stories for Every Day."

(3) Generosity

" Why the Chimes Rang," parable-story, teaching that the chief thing in any giving is the attitude of the giver. Telling-time, about fifteen minutes. Alden.

6. Senior Period, Ages about Fifteen to Seventeen

(1) Ambition

" The Boy Who Wanted to be a School Teacher, Antonio Canova," history-story, teaching that initiative in making the most of an opportunity may lead to the realization of a worthy ambition. Telling-time, about six minutes. Found in " For the Children's Hour, Book Three."

(2) Appreciation

" The Great Stone Face," parable-story, teaching that we tend to become like that which we value most. Telling-time, about five minutes. Found in " World Stories Retold."

(3) Industry

" The Jew's Tale," legend-story, teaching that success is attained by unceasing toil, and not by magic. Telling-time, about ten minutes. Found in " World Stories Retold."

7. Young People's Period, Ages about Eighteen to Twenty-four

(1) Marriage

"Ruth and Boaz," history-story, teaching that courtship and marriage are of fundamental importance in the building of a nation. Telling-time, about fifteen minutes. Found in the Bible.

(2) Parenthood

" Cornelia and Her Jewels," history-story, teaching that children are of supreme value in the home and in society. Telling-time, about seven minutes. Found in " World Stories Retold."

(3) Service

Tolstoy's " Martin the Cobbler," parable-story, teaching that Christ seems nearest to those who best serve their fellow-beings. Telling-time, about ten minutes. Found in " World Stories Retold."

READING AND DISCUSSION

1. Analyze and re-list five of the stories listed in " A Manual of Stories," by Forbush.

2. Analyze and re-list five of the stories in " Story Telling for Upper Grade Teachers," by Cross and Statler.

3. Analyze and re-list five stories listed in some other book.

4. State your chief difficulty in analyzing and listing a story.

5. Give five reasons for analyzing and listing stories.

Printed in the United States
122715LV00004B/253/A

9 781419 113796